WRITING SPIRITUAL BOOKS

Writing Spiritual Books

A Bestselling Writer's Guide to Successful Publication

HAL ZINA BENNETT

Inner Ocean Publishing, Inc.
Maui, Hawai'i • San Francisco, California

Inner Ocean Publishing, Inc.
P.O. Box 1239
Makawao, Maui, HI 96768-1239
www.innerocean.com

Printed on recycled paper

Publisher Cataloging-in-Publication Data

Bennett, Hal Zina, 1936-
Writing spiritual books : a bestselling writer's guide to successful publication / Hal Zina Bennett. — Makawao, Hawaii : Inner Ocean, 2004.

p. ; cm.

ISBN: 1-930722-37-0
1. Religious literature—Authorship. 2. Authorship—Style manuals. 3. Authorship—Marketing. 4. Religious literature—Marketing. 5. Spirituality. I. Title.

BR44 .B46 2004
808/.0662—dc22 0411

DISTRIBUTED BY PUBLISHERS GROUP WEST

For information on promotions, bulk purchases, premiums, or educational use, please contact: 866.731.2216 or sales@innerocean.com.

For my students and clients,

to assure them their lessons

were not lost on me.

Contents

Acknowledgments

Writing and publishing a book is the work of a great many people, something that's not easy to see as we hold the finished product in our hands. Only the author's name is on the cover. But getting the book to you, the reader, involves literary agent, editor, book designers, assistants of various kinds, the secretaries that answer the phones, the librarian who checks facts, the printers, the sales reps, the distributors, the bookstore owners, and finally you, the reader.

And what would any of us not give for a sound support group at home—Susan, our dogs Maddy and Cicely, and K.C. the maniac cat whose favorite trick is to leap on my keyboard at the most inappropriate moments. (She knows!)

Thanking everyone is always a daunting task since inevitably someone's name gets left out, not because their contribution went unnoticed but because the author's memory failed him that day. Risking all that, I'd like to thank the following people, more or less in the order they became involved in this project: First and foremost, I want to thank all my students and clients whose challenges motivated me to seek answers that I'd later share with others.

Thank you, Barbara Neighbors Deal, my literary agent and friend, whose focus on higher purposes helps me keep my priorities straight.

Roger Jellinek, editor, writer, and literary agent, guided me through several revisions of the original plan for this book, ultimately improving it immensely.

Next came Karen Bouris, publisher at Inner Ocean, and a fellow author. Her rare combination of humor, firmness, and skill kept things on track and made it fun.

For the second time in my career, I've been blessed with the fine artistry of Kathy Warriner, book designer extraordinnaire.

Thanks, Heather McArthur, whose editorial suggestions for improving the manuscript were golden.

And where would I be without a good copyeditor? We authors are blind to typos and misspellings (sic). So I owe a debt of gratitude to Valerie Sinzdak for an eye much sharper than my own.

Last but certainly not least, I thank the *Wiz* who keeps my soul searching and the ink flowing.

Introduction

I remember as a child of four or five asking my mother, "Where did I come from?" The answer I got was anything but satisfactory. I was told that babies were born out of the mother's body. This I already knew, of course, since I had seen my aunt's belly get big and was told there was a baby in there. I tried asking my question another way: "Why did I come into the family I did? If I hadn't come to this family, where would I have gone? What was I before I was born?" My parents shrugged and smiled when I asked these questions. But my questioning continued.

At first I sought answers to these mysteries in the woods and open fields around our home. I found a dead bird one day and held it in my hand. Clearly the life was gone from this tiny fragile body. But how could that be? Where did that life go? Could it come back? I'm told I was six or seven years old at that time. I placed the bird in a cardboard box, with air holes I'd punched in the cover. Every morning, and several times a day, I opened the box to see if life had returned to the bird. Of course, it didn't, and in time my parents suggested that I bury it, which I did, even placing a stone on its grave to mark where it lay.

There were times when I thought I saw things very clearly, when the veils of everyday life seemed to lift, revealing a truth about my own life and life around me that even today defies words. But the mystery I pursued always felt just beyond my reach, sometimes so close I felt my heart lift ecstatically. I didn't know what any of this was, nor could I even talk to others about it since nothing I said seemed to communicate what I was experiencing.

When I first considered writing this book, those early childhood memories came back to me. I realized that the questions I was now asking as an adult were the same as those I'd asked as a child. I did not know it as a child, nor were there people around me who were able to put words to it, but even at that tender age I was aware of the spiritual. And regardless of how intangible it might be, I knew it was real.

As I recalled those experiences, I realized that things hadn't changed all that much, even to this day. Hardly a day passes that I don't stop with wonder and ask pretty much the same questions I asked at six and seven and eight. But I also know that I'm not alone in this. I doubt there is a person alive who has not, however fleetingly, been touched by those spiritual breakthroughs that cause us to look with new eyes on the meaning of our lives.

Today I've learned the contentment of living with a deep inner peace around my questions, no longer requiring the answers but knowing it's enough to bask in the mystery. I suppose this position was what caused the initial resistance I felt to writing this book. Many people from my workshops had urged me to write the book, though I don't think I began to take it seriously until I'd heard the same suggestion for about the hundredth time. My resistance had to do with my belief that there is something almost arrogant about presuming to have the words to speak of the spiritual. It took me years, at least five, to get over my resistance and actually sit down to work out the problems this book posed for me.

The breakthrough for me came when I realized that you, the reader, would bring to your writing the material you would be teaching with your words. All I had to do was show you the ropes of how to put a spiritual book together. I started asking some new questions: How was a spiritual book different than any other nonfiction book one might write? Were there aspects of a spiritual book that were different from a nonfiction book on any other subject, say a book about organic gardening or health? Yes, I decided, there were differences. I knew this from having written a number of spiritual books and from helping other authors write them. And so I set out to define those differences and explore them in a book—this book.

First and foremost are the deeply personal experiences that we bring to the writing of a book on spirituality. I'd learned from teaching classes that these highly individualized experiences were also where we touched others, often striking a universal chord. That is one of life's greatest contradictions, that what is the most personal can also reach into other people's lives and get them in touch with the truth of our oneness. Thus, we need to know how to reach into ourselves and describe what is nearest and dearest for us.

Second was the realization that we best speak of the spiritual after we've established a particular relationship with our readers. Because readers feel the integrity of an author's spiritual experience through his or her words, and through what we are willing to share with them about our lives, we cannot hide our hearts from our readers. At least where the subject of our book is concerned, we need to disclose enough about our own thoughts, feelings, and experiences to convince our readers that we are as passionately involved in our material as we might wish them to be.

Third, the subject of spirituality does not always reveal itself in linear or scientific processes. The spiritual exists in a space that extends out in all directions. Thus, in attempting to organize one's ideas and experiences, I turned to a system called *mind mapping*, or *clustering*, that allows our minds to expand outward even as we develop a format for writing our books.

Fourth, while the spiritual writing we might do for ourselves, often in our journals, is deeply personal, it may or may not be important to others. When it comes to writing a book, we must acknowledge the *other*. We are no longer just recording our own experiences but are entering into a rather intimate relationship with our readers. To address this, I started looking at the responsibilities we take on as authors when we write about themes that reach deeply into our readers' hearts and souls. I weave my insights about those responsibilities throughout the book.

Fifth, I looked at the fact that many times readers come to spiritual books for confirmation to erase their own doubts. Especially in the early stages of opening to Spirit, we look for proof and find it elusive. So, it is my belief that in writing a spiritual book, the doubt and hesitation readers may feel has to be addressed in a way that fosters trust even when tangible proof is unavailable.

Finally, despite the many differences between spiritual books and other nonfiction, there are also certain realities about writing anything for publication, and I knew I had to bring those into the mix. Writing is not just about craft. Publishing a book is ultimately a community effort, involving the work of many others—editors, book designers, proofreaders, printers, sales reps, booksellers, and finally readers. I've tried to provide a kind of map through the process of writing and publishing a book, and even beyond that into the marketing and promotion of the book. For this you'll find a large "Resources" section, a place to go to find the help you need to take each new step along the way.

As I came to the final pages of writing this book, doubts about my efforts to share my knowledge began to fade. I felt myself buoyed up by an image of this book helping to inspire people who want to write and fostering courage by providing good tools and resources for success. It excites me to imagine people who are on a spiritual path bringing their own wisdom to the world through the assistance of this book. Writing books of this kind is more important than ever, for there are great changes going on in the world that require us to speak out about the truth we see beyond the veils of everyday travail. I hope this small book might help you manifest your dreams of sharing your vision.

How to Use This Book

As you sit down to read this book, you may be at the beginning, middle, or end of writing your book. You may have already read other books about writing and publishing and thus have a pretty good idea about what you need to do next. Because it is impossible for me to anticipate where you might be in the process, I have written this book so that each chapter and the information in it can stand alone. For that reason, I suggest that you study the table of contents and see if one of the chapters pops out at you, answering an immediate need that you have. If that happens, by all means follow the tug of your interests. If chapter ten, "Getting Published and What Comes After," leaps out at you, start there. If you're drawn to chapter six, "Fostering Receptivity and Change," start there.

Treat the book as a personal reference guiding you through all the processes, from writing to finished book. Keep it on your shelf in a place where you can easily find it, so if questions arise you'll have the guidance handy.

Finally, note the "Resources" section that I've provided. Turn to it early on and peruse what's there. You might find that you want to start exploring some of these resources even though you have just begun writing your book. For example, you might want to start querying literary agents. Or maybe you can begin exploring publishers to see what's available. You'll want to start researching what particular publishers are seeking.

Get to know the book. Peruse it broadly. And then start in reading wherever your interests and your present needs take you.

Chapter One

Writing in Spirit

The only books that influence us are those for which we are ready, and which have gone a little further down our particular path than we have gone ourselves.

—E.M. Forster, *Longest Journey*, 1907

Writing a spiritual book at times presents us with wild contradictions. How can words possibly duplicate the awe, or even ecstasy, that wells up in us as we lift the veils of our everyday world and catch a glimpse of the spiritual aspects of life? We find ourselves reaching, even yearning, for something that cannot be described or named, yet is made no less real by our inability to encompass it with words.

Throughout the millennia, spiritual teachers have avoided words, or used them sparingly, favoring object lessons instead. For example, there's the traditional story of the Buddhist master who whacks his students on the head with a stick, forcing them to come into the *now*. As a Buddhist friend once remarked, "The wisdom of that stick outshines the power of thought." What he referred to was the fact that approaching the spiritual only from our intellects distances us from the present. The pain of that firm but harmless whack on the head brings us back into the *now*, which is exactly where we must be to encounter the spiritual.

Ironically, the more we come to know the spiritual, the more frustrating it can be to express it with words, regardless of our skills with language. We can no more capture the spiritual with words than we can paint or draw the wind. But we can suggest the presence of the wind with flowing lines or swipes of paint on canvas. Similarly, we can suggest the presence of the spiritual by offering anecdotes of other people's experiences, or our own. By entering these experiences voyeuristically, readers essentially borrow the author's eyes to view an aspect of their own lives that was invisible until then.

To accomplish these ends, we sometimes borrow the craft of the poet or novelist, conveying to our readers not just factual information but sensory and emotional information as well. For that reason, we might be advised to study how poets and novelists immerse their readers in the author's experiences, or in the experiences of a person the author wishes to tell us about. Some people call these techniques "creative nonfiction," since they call upon the creative and imaginative powers of the writer.

I am not speaking here of creating make-believe worlds so much as using the writing techniques of creative writers. The key is in describing what you sense, that is, what you see, hear, taste, smell, touch, and feel (emotionally) rather than only what you think. There is a strange irony in this, is there not, since logic would tell us that abstraction and the intellect, more than our physical senses, would carry us into the spiritual? But like counting breaths in meditation, these tricks of the pen often reveal to us the truths that reality obscures.

When writing in our journals about the spiritual work we're doing, or the epiphanies we've had as a result of that work, it's not unusual to find that we have used physical descriptions and even dialogue to capture those experiences. After all, we understand the world only by first encountering it through our senses. Go back and review your journals. Look for passages where your descriptions were particularly vivid and effective. It just might be that you are already quite adept with this kind of writing. If not, have patience: we'll be exploring many such techniques in the pages ahead.

Putting Your Readers into the Picture

Another way to write about the spiritual is to describe ways your readers can experience it for themselves. After all, what's better than firsthand experience? *Experiential exercises*, as they are called, put your readers into situations where they are most likely to get what we are saying not through our explanations but by their own feelings and senses. I am reminded here of something that happened several years ago, while teaching a writing workshop at Mount Shasta, in Northern California. As anyone who has ever spent much time there knows, Mount Shasta is a spectacular formation, rising over 14,000 feet into the sky. Most of the year her peaks are crowned in snow; by October she is completely blanketed in white, down to about the 3,000-foot elevation. The breathtaking beauty and spiritual power of Mount Shasta are often compared to Japan's Fujiyama, recognized by many as her sister mountain. Both are known for their ability to awaken visitors to the spiritual dimensions of all life.

My visit to Mount Shasta was in the spring, with bracing winds still sweeping down from the snowy peaks. From the place where I was teaching, the mountain dominated the skyline, a view that ordinarily left me in sublime awe. But on that weekend, this same view aroused a sense of sadness. I simply could not connect with it as I had done in the past. To me it might as well have been a painted backdrop on a movie set. Between a heavy writing and teaching schedule, I'd been feeling there was no space in my life for taking in the joys of the present. I hadn't even taken time to reflect on personal issues that had been piling up. (All of this was a great contradiction, of course, since these were the issues I was teaching.) As a result, my life had been reduced to meeting the demands of my too-busy schedule. There was no time for creative endeavors. I felt completely out of touch with Spirit.

As the class was breaking up and people were packing their cars to leave, I overheard Robyn, one of the women from the workshop, talking with two others about a shamanic process she'd learned at a workshop she'd recently attended. It was a reflective technique that she'd found very useful. She said that it helped her get in touch with thoughts and feelings that had been blocking her and that it was great preparation for vision-questing or for a daily meditation practice. I was eager to find out about this exercise, hoping it might guide me into a reflective space where I might sort out some of the things that had been troubling me.

I excused myself for eavesdropping and asked Robyn if she had the time before she left to show me this technique. She answered yes. She was planning to stay in the area for two more days and would be glad to do just that. Immediately, the two women she'd been speaking with asked if they could join us and said they were planning to stay through the next day. I had things I had to do the next morning, so we made plans to meet in the afternoon.

At three the next day, we met at the high school parking lot and drove up the mountain together in Robyn's SUV. We stopped at about 8,000 feet and headed out along one of the less-used trails. Robyn said we should each find a place to sit alone and meditate. I was very much looking forward to this, regardless of what other skills she might bring to the experience. She promised that after a certain time had passed, she would come around and work with each of us individually.

I'd climbed for a half hour or so when I stopped to catch my breath. The place where I stopped offered a spectacular view of the mountain. Dense white clouds nuzzled the distant crests against a deep blue sky. In that special moment, I could remind myself that all the tensions I'd been carrying for the past several weeks were just beliefs and feelings I had created and was holding onto. As real as my problems might be, it was clear they did not need to consume me. While I could see this was true, my *monkey mind* continued to chatter away, keeping me focused more on the past and future than on the present.

Nearly an hour passed as I sat atop a great rock waiting for Robyn to show up. I started wondering why she was taking so long. I knew two other people were involved, though this did not satisfy me. My mind was going a mile a minute, refusing to slow down what had become my habitual pace. Maybe Robyn had been unable to find me. Maybe I'd gone further up the trail than she'd intended us to go. Maybe I should return to the car. What if the others had already finished and were waiting for me?

I became so distracted by the waiting that I could not even focus on the issues that had brought me here. I saw the irony in all this but was helpless to do anything about it.

At last Robyn showed up. She asked how I was doing and I admitted that I'd been too distracted to meditate or even begin to stop my busy mind from chattering away incessantly. Her response to this admission took me completely off guard.

"Go find a rock," she said. "Something around the size of a loaf of bread or slightly smaller."

"Just any rock?"

"Choose one you can easily hold . . . one that appeals to you."

I was feeling dubious and began to regret having come on this escapade. What could this possibly have to do with personal reflection and clearing my mind of distractions! Nevertheless, for the next few moments I wandered around looking for a rock that appealed to me and that met the criteria Robyn had described. I brought it back to the place I'd been sitting and took out the pencil and small notebook she'd instructed me to bring.

"Now, turn the rock several times, looking at it from all angles," Robyn instructed. "When you are ready, stop, study the surface facing you, and describe anything you see. When you've seen something, quickly write it down in your notebook, just a word or two, then turn the rock ninety degrees and repeat the process."

Over the next twenty minutes or so, I did as she instructed. On the first side of the rock I saw only a kind of trail, in miniature, working through the rock. It might have been a trail in the mountains: "Precipitous trail," I wrote.

I turned the rock ninety degrees. Now I saw a cat, perhaps a puma, stalking its game. I wrote: "Puma hunting."

Twice more I turned the rock and recorded what I imagined seeing in its veins and configurations. That done, Robyn asked me to go back to my notes, and use the rock as my reference to revisit what I'd written down. She then left me and walked back down the trail, presumably to spend time by herself.

I do not know how much time passed, but as I worked with the stone, expanding on my notes, I became immersed in my reflections, easily focusing my attention on the images I'd seen in the rock. Not unsurprisingly, they all related directly to the issues that had been piling up in my inner life over the past several weeks. Truly, I had been feeling like I was treading a "precipitous path." The images I projected to the rock were telling me much about the broader, more spiritual dimensions of the problems I was encountering. Most had to do with personal changes I was facing in my life. Others were more mundane, each one a small matter that, if approached individually, had a relatively quick solution. I soon realized that the accumulation of all these small issues had led to my feeling overwhelmed. The imagery I found in the rock helped me to more clearly see what I had to do.

When I at last looked up, I had my bearings and could take action to resolve the issues that had been troubling me. I knew where I was going with them and felt confident in my ability to proceed. I set aside the rock and my notebook and looked around me. My mind was no longer cluttered. A sense of solitude and contentment came over me. A tiny bird fluttered in and settled down on my rock, less than two feet away. It stayed for only a second, chirped, then flew away. For that moment, it seemed to relate to me as just another animal in the landscape.

I began to notice other small animals, chipmunks, a squirrel, birds overhead. Had they been there before I'd worked with the rock? If they were, I hadn't noticed them. For several minutes I sat there, enjoying this moment of communion with the animals, the rocks, the mountain, the sky, and the sparse vegetation. Immersed in the landscape, I felt so much a part of it that the thought of leaving filled me with regret. However, the sky was growing dark and I became concerned about the others who might be waiting for me.

I carried my rock back to the place where I'd found it, as per Robyn's instructions, thanked it for its service, then made my way back down the trail to the car where, indeed, my friends were waiting for me.

Over dinner at a restaurant in town, we shared our experiences, with Robyn answering our many questions. Several things became clear to me that day: First, that this process had been tremendously helpful in allowing me to get focused on issues that had been preoccupying me for days; second, when I finally addressed those issues, I was able to be in a contemplative space in my being that allowed me to be present with the mountain and all the small beings who made it their home.

The tiny bird who had settled on the rock so close to me had made me feel that I had made a definite shift of consciousness that even the animals noticed. Certainly I was feeling more at one with the world around me. Was it possible they had felt this about me as well?

As I look back on that day, I am reminded of how important tools and exercises such as this can be. The rock definitely helped focus my attention, allowing me to reflect calmly on everything that had been piling up in my mind. The rock had become a mirror of my inner world, allowing me to come to terms with the challenges that lay ahead.

As you were reading the previous passages, with Robyn guiding me through the process with the rock, you might have noticed that I wasn't the only one learning how to do it. So were you! If you wished to, you could probably repeat it for yourself, based on what you just read. Simultaneously, you were experiencing a little bit of what I was going through—what I was feeling, thinking, sensing all around me, and learning. What just happened here is that I took you into my own learning experience, using the craft of the novelist and poet—such as physical description, character description, and dialogue—even as I was giving you enough description to do the rock exercise and experience it for yourself firsthand. And, yes, for the record, this really did happen.

You can effectively guide your readers into the spiritual realm through anecdotes about other people, by sharing experiences of your own, by describing exercises for experiencing what you're talking about firsthand, or through a combination of all three.

More than with most types of books, you'll want to keep in mind that you are taking your readers into territories that many may not yet be comfortable with, and thus they've been reluctant to venture too far on their own. There's a certain responsibility in what you are writing; of that we should all be aware. What's often not obvious to us as writers is that readers have entered into an unspoken agreement with us. Readers appreciate authors who seem able to understand and support the processes of change and expansion that they, the readers, might be going through. As authors, we need to be conscious of this. We need to build upon and honor the trust our readers have placed in us.

Contracts Between Readers and Writers

Way back when I was studying creative writing at the university, there were lively debates about whether or not there was an implied contract between author and reader. The arguments covered a wide spectrum, from writers who believed that their only contract was to be true to their own creative gifts, to those who believed that our only responsibility was to not disappoint our readers. The latter was pretty self-evident, since authors who disappoint their readers are soon looking for other work.

No doubt there was some truth in those arguments we defended so passionately back at the university, but as the years passed—now more than thirty—it has become obvious that life teaches us lessons we aren't ready to hear when we're sophomores in creative writing school. Chief among those things we learn is the implied contract we have in every human interaction, whether it is writing a book or buying stamps at the post office. If we're buying stamps, the implied contract is that our interactions with the clerk will result in an exchange of like values—stamps for money. If we're choosing a book to read, the implied contract can be found in what the book promises and how well the author fulfills that promise.

What exactly is the promise? In a mystery book, the contract might be that the author will keep us guessing and provide a satisfying resolution. In a book about American history, the contract might be to deliver in an interesting way some semblance of truth about what has gone before us. In a book about how to run a software program, the implied contract is that we will be better at running our computers. And so it goes. But spiritual writing often involves a contract that goes much deeper, and is perhaps less obvious than any of these.

A spiritual book often delves into places that are deeply personal and even precious to us. Because of the intimate nature of spiritual writing, writers need to be aware of the depth to which they might be going with their readers. These books can and do change lives, and that's not to be taken lightly. A woman in one of my workshops suggested that it is like proclaiming our love to another person. In both cases—falling in love or writing a spiritual book—we need to really mean what we say and take our readers' lives at least as seriously as we take our subject matter.

In any discussion of our spiritual lives there are at least three entities involved: you, me, and a presence greater than all of us. That third entity is part of the equation in whatever we write. There's a line from the Bible that has always impressed me: "Where two or three are gathered together in my name, there am I in the midst of them" (Matthew 18:20). In the passage's original context, it was Jesus, representing the Word of God that would be in their midst. But whether you're a Christian, Jew, Muslim, Zuni, or Buddhist, or you follow any of the infinite paradigms that guide spiritual thought, the deeper meaning is not attached to any specific person or belief system. What's ultimately implied is that somehow in our gathering together we touch our common source, that is, our oneness. Gregory Bateson is said to have stated it thusly: "It takes two to know one." [1]

It seems to me that in virtually every spiritual book, it is this "one" that we are striving to join with. What we can count on as we sit down to write is that we share with our readers this desire to connect with Spirit. That's what your readers want from the synergy that they establish with you when they sit down to read your book. Unlike other writing, however, there is this third "voice" involved, whatever name you might call it—God, Allah, Jesus, Buddha, Moses, Mohammed, The Word, etc. Ultimately, the message we communicate in a spiritual book is not just our own but a glimpse beyond the veil of everyday reality, a glimpse of the One.

The Perennial Philosophy: Key Spiritual Principles

A number of years ago, someone in a seminar remarked that he believed there were universal themes that were part of every spiritual teaching. Though he couldn't define these themes for himself, he was convinced they were there. He thought it important to have some grasp of these themes if we were going to be writing books in this genre. The answer I gave at the time was to explore what Aldous Huxley had written about the "perennial philosophy."[2]

Huxley helped to popularize work that was originally expressed by German philosopher Gottfried Wilhelm Leibniz in the 17th century. Leibniz had stated that there are four fundamental concepts that form the foundation of all philosophies, religions, and spiritual practice, both Eastern and Western. These concepts reflect not only what motivates an author to write spiritual books but also what motivates our readers to be seekers on the spiritual path. I paraphrase Huxley's words below. The following are the four principles of the perennial philosophy:

1. The *phenomenal world*—that is, the entire world we perceive through our five senses, including ourselves, all other creatures, and all matter and all form of being—is inseparable from Divine Ground. To be other than Divine Ground is impossible, for Divine Ground is all that exists. While we may have illusions of being separate from it, this cannot be since nothing can exist apart from Divine Ground.

2. We humans are able to not only know *about* the Divine Ground—that is, to be able to grasp it intellectually—but are also able to experience it directly, through direct knowing, or intuition, in this way uniting knower with known. When we

experience this unity, or oneness, our dualistic illusions (that we are separate from spirit) fade away and we have no sense of separation from Spirit or Divine Ground. We literally find our *grounding* in the Divine.

3. We all possess a double nature: an *ego self,* which operates within the physical world of the senses (the phenomenal world), and an *eternal self,* which is identified with Divine Ground. The eternal self (spirit) is, in fact, inseparable from Divine Ground, and we can choose to identify with this part of our being or with the ego self. If we identify with the latter, we perceive ourselves as only a separate being existing within the phenomenal world.

4. Our ultimate purpose on Earth is to identify with the eternal self and experience coming into oneness with the Divine Ground.

As you write, remind yourself of these four principles and note how they turn up in your writing. This doesn't mean that you necessarily find yourself quoting or even paraphrasing these statements, but that if you search far enough you will find they are keystones in the foundation of virtually anything we might say about our spirituality. I've found that the awareness of these principles helps me to keep whatever I write focused and clear.

Going Forward

As you read the chapters ahead, the subjects we've discussed here will become increasingly clear, as will their application in the writing of a spiritual book. What you will discover along the way is that your motives for this kind of writing bring you more fully in alignment with these principles. You will also find that your own interests will translate easily into your readers' interests, with the form and style of your book evolving in a way that is completely compatible with what you wish to write.

Chapter Two

From Revelation to Publication

The wonderful thing about books is that they allow us to enter imaginatively into someone else's life. And when we do that, we learn to sympathize with other people. But the real surprise is that we also learn truths about ourselves, about our own lives, that somehow we hadn't been able to see before.

—Katherine Paterson, *The Horn Book*

When we first sit down to write a book, our passion for our material drives us. Surely, that is the way it should be. That passion might even carry us through the writing of a complete manuscript before we ever look at what might be involved in publishing. It's only then that we begin to see that publishing has its own set of requirements that don't always seem compatible with what we've just written. Many writers I've worked with find it difficult to come to terms with what can seem like a great disparity between the writer's and the publisher's worlds. Recognizing the difficulties of building a bridge between these two worlds, I decided to take that task on right away, here in chapter two, so that what comes after this chapter could be understood through this lens. The good news is that the bridges between writers and publishers of spiritual books is getting a little easier to traverse since more publishers than ever before are finding it profitable. This is a reminder to us that publishing is, after all, a business, and as often as not this means that making money is the bottom line.

While making money is not what motivates most of us who write for the spiritual market, it's certainly nice to think that the potential is there to support our efforts. There has never been a time in history when spiritual writings were more in demand, be it in magazine articles or books. What's more, writing has become an integral part of thousands of people's spiritual path, with workshops and weekly discussion groups centering on participants being able to share and discuss entries from their private journals. From the publisher's perspective, having a lot of people interested in spiritual development means there's a market worth going after. Sounds crass, I suppose, but that's the way it is. From the writer's perspective, it means having a readership with whom we can openly share ideas and experiences that are important to us.

Along with an expanding readership for spiritual writing, we also have an expanding number of reasons that bring people to such writings. Readers might be motivated by a search for meaning at a time of personal crisis. They might be afraid because of threatening global unrest. They could have had a recent breakthrough experience of their own. They might want to bring spiritual values into the workplace, or they could simply want to create a better life for themselves.

As writers, there comes a point when, if we wish to publish, we have to start asking ourselves, "Who is my reader? What is the best way for me to focus what I've written so that it reaches the people I want to reach?" Put simply, this means, instead of trying to be all things to all people, think about your readers' needs, that is, what they are seeking and why they might be attracted, or not attracted, to what you've written. You or I might want to focus on, say, people who follow Buddhist principles, who are managers in large corporations, and who are looking for ways to use these principles at work. That's sharply focused, for certain, but is the readership we've carved out for ourselves big enough for a publisher to bother publishing a book about it? To answer that, you need to identify your niche.

How Big Is Your Niche?

One of the realities we face when we start looking at publishing is the size of the potential readership we're writing to. This doesn't mean you should change the way you're writing your book in order to reach a broader market—though, indeed, that might be a choice you'd make. But it does mean being realistic about the size of your potential readership and what you can do to more sharply focus your writings for the people you want to reach. If you have a very narrow readership focus, consider self-publishing, or going with a publishing house that specializes in the narrow niche you're considering. Understand that you might be talking about selling only a few hundred or a couple thousand books. Fortunately, in this day and age, you can actually do okay with small niches like this. New printing technologies make it so.

Estimating the size of your niche isn't easy, however. One way to estimate it is to explore media venues that might be available for you to publish an article on the subject you're interested in, or where you might buy an ad for your book. For example, let's say you are writing a book on shamanism. You might go to the library and look at a periodicals catalog to find the titles and addresses of magazines that specialize in articles on shamanism. Then email the magazines and ask for advertising information. Be sure to ask what their circulation is. I recently did this, finding two leading magazines that specialize in shamanistic material: *Shamans Drum* in the United States and *Sacred Hoop* in England. Their combined circulations are under 20,000 copies. For the sake of giving some perspective on the sizes of niches, I looked up information on magazines for private pilots. There are seven magazines catering to private pilots that I've found through a quick Internet search. Their combined circulation is well over 2.5 million.

Tracking down magazine circulation figures is relatively easy to do with the Internet. Since there are magazines on virtually every topic, you can usually find one or two in whatever niche you're interested in and get information about them online in a matter of minutes. Magazines are required to make circulation numbers available to advertisers. And while these numbers are not necessarily accurate predictors of how many books you'll sell to that niche, they will at least give you a rough idea of what's out there.

Often in workshops, people seem surprised to learn that most published books sell somewhere between 3,000 and 20,000 copies. There's a widespread belief that anytime you publish a book you reach millions of people. That's rare. If you read best-seller lists, you might get a very different impression, since books on spiritual subjects published by mainstream houses sometimes sell in the millions of copies, making their authors' names household words, seemingly overnight. But that's much more the exception than the rule, accounting for a very small percentage of the books published.

Hundreds of authors make important contributions through their writings by publishing with smaller, independent houses and reaching a slightly more modest but enthusiastic readership. And then there are the self-published authors whose spiritual books find their own appreciative groups of readers; now and then, these books even turn up on bestseller lists.

The commercial success of spiritual books can indeed be rewarding, don't get me wrong. And what could be better than writing a successful book on a subject you love and that's such an important part of your life! But for most of us writing in this genre, money is not the main motivation. If my own experience as an author and writing coach has taught me anything, it is that most people interested in writing for this readership do so because they are passionately committed to sharing what life has taught them. Sometimes the act of writing is reward enough, for we've found that our words put us in touch with our hearts, our minds, and our souls, deepening, affirming, and expanding the spiritual journey. The power of words can carry us beyond our everyday limitations into realities where the wisdom of our hearts enriches what we might otherwise know only through our intellects and senses.

What Makes a Good Writer?

Do you have to be a professional writer to write a successful spiritual book? No. Many writers, even those who've written bestsellers, did not start out as writers. When I think about the hundreds of people I've known who write about spiritual subjects, I can only think of two or three who aspired to become an author. For the rest, even those who went on to publish very successful books, a life-changing experience motivated them to write: for one person, this happened after a trip to Nepal; for another, after surviving a car wreck; for another, after surviving a life-threatening disease; for another, after losing a child; for another, after a near-death experience; for another, after recovering from alcoholism; and for still another, after visiting a third world country and witnessing the deep and loving relationships people enjoyed even in the midst of great poverty.

Is it always a dramatic event such as these that brings one to a spiritual view of the world, and then into wanting to write about it? Not at all. But I do know that the breakthrough experiences that open us up to other dimensions of reality always have their own subtle dramas, regardless of the external circumstances that seemed to trigger them. As often as not, we are introduced to the spiritual through reading a passage in a book, hearing a lecture, experiencing a deep meditation, or spending time in nature. The significant part of any of these experiences is how the insight or vision we have changes us inside and then changes our relationships with the world around us.

While a dramatic incident such as surviving a life-threatening car wreck might make a good story, if we don't get to an underlying spiritual message that we can relate to, it's *only* a story. At first we may turn to writing in a private journal in an effort to comprehend or clarify the message for ourselves. Or maybe we just want to make sure we don't forget what we've experienced, sort of like keeping a scrapbook of meaningful events in our lives. Or maybe we turn to writing because the spiritual experience we've had has triggered a crisis in our own belief system—what authors Stan and Christina Grof call a "spiritual emergency"[1]—and we find that writing helps us to grow through that crisis and come to terms with how our lives have changed.

In my own case, a life-threatening disease and near-death experience, followed by a period of blindness, provided insights that I would struggle with for at least ten years before I even began to come to terms with them. During that time, I filled notebooks with my meandering thoughts, kept dream journals, recorded conversations I had with myself, as well as with dream figures and real people; I recorded sessions with my psychotherapists of the time and collected quotes from books I'd been reading. The journals themselves were important to me, but they were a mishmash of writings that often had no continuity from one page to the next. They meant a lot to me personally, but very little to others.

I have to say, however, that while some of that personal writing may have survived long enough to make it into one or more of the books I've written, most didn't. And yet, when I read passages from my books, I find the lessons of those earlier writings, still very much alive between the lines, reminding me that sometimes what makes it into print owes a great debt to what didn't and maybe never will.

It is important to recognize these kinds of experiences as our real *credentials.* Though they may not be recognized by the university system, they do qualify us to write a spiritual book. It's the good inner work we've done, even more than the little initials we get to put after our names for completing a college program, that most readers on a spiritual path will respond to.

Honor the life experiences that are the basis for your private writings and never underestimate their importance. Take the time to understand the role these experiences play in your life, a role that, in the final analysis, helps to define the person you are. Understand that we are never more generous than when we give of ourselves, and this kind of giving comes out of the lives we've lived and what we've done with the gifts we've received both through our challenges and our joys.

As for the process of getting from point A to point B in our writing—that is, from our life experiences to a successful book or article—that journey is not always an easy one, though I have found it gets easier when we understand the value of sharing what has come out of our own lives. Based on what I've seen, both as an author and as a writing coach, our real credentials are found within, in the journey from self-recognition to recognizing our oneness with all sentient beings—particularly those who read, of course.

Authenticity and Responsibility

There is great value in making spiritual writing a regular part of your personal practice, whether it's for yourself, a handful of friends, for people in a workshop you are teaching, or for a large general readership. For many of us, whether we're thinking of publishing or not, writing takes us deeper into ourselves, into a place that is beyond the demands and constraints of our egos. At its best, language can produce what the ancient Celts called "thin places," that is, places or moments in life when the curtain between physical and spiritual worlds is swept aside, allowing us to peer out, past everyday reality, and catch a glimpse of the Divine. It's here that we feel the full impact of our spiritual identity. These thin places might be awe-inspiring places we visited in nature, "sacred sites" whose beauty is so breathtaking that we are literally taken out of ourselves. Thin places might also be created in poetry, music, or dance. Or we might find them in the great cathedrals of Europe, the mosques of the Middle East, and the softly austere temples of Asia—all of them imparting a sense of wonder and mystery. When they are most effective, spiritual writings lead us, as well as our readers, to that place where we may, in our solitude, encounter the *mystery* and be filled by it.

Because of the transcendent nature of the better spiritual books, writing them can be more demanding than writing books on other subjects. For one thing, if we are to fully engage our readers and have them seriously consider our observations or teachings, we need to speak not just to the intellect but to the body and spirit. Spiritual writing, being deeply inward, must be based on firsthand experience. It's not something a writer can fake, the way a science fiction writer might fake a trip to another planet by reading scenes from another writer's books or going to a movie. In a spiritual book, we must speak from the heart and draw directly from life, with an understanding that to be effective, our message must be transmitted from our hearts and souls and received by the hearts and souls of our readers.

This is a tall order, of course. It implies that we've accepted a certain responsibility with our readers. As a reminder of this, there's a line by Ralph Waldo Emerson that I keep tacked on the wall behind my computer. Emerson tells us: "'Tis the good reader that makes the good book. . . . The profoundest thought or passage sleeps as in a mine, until it is discovered by an equal mind and heart." It's true that readers themselves must bring something to the writing. It's equally true that if we're to succeed in our efforts we must offer our readers knowledge that has been tested through our own life experiences—and therein lies the greatest responsibility. To use Emerson's metaphor of the mine, we must not only point readers to the mother lode but also supply them with the tools and the light to uncover the treasure.

As a writing coach and editor, I've noticed that this is one of the more difficult lessons for writers to master. Getting facts down on paper isn't enough. More than that, we have to get them down in such a way that our readers can take them in with the same enthusiasm, depth, and excitement the author intended. Whenever I'm teaching this point in a workshop, there's invariably someone who argues: "I say what I want to say as clearly as I can. Beyond that, readers have to take responsibility for whatever they're going to get out of it."

"I partially agree with you. But let me ask you this," I'll often say. "If you want to communicate an important piece of information to a friend in another room, is it enough to just state it and let it go at that?"

"Well, if it was really important, I'd want some acknowledgment that they've heard me, of course."

"How would that happen?"

"By them saying okay or something."

"And if they didn't say it?"

"I might ask them if they'd heard me."

"So it's important to you that your friend in the next room hears and understands you. Shouldn't you be just as concerned about your readers?"

"But I'm not there with the reader!"

Of course, that's the challenge, isn't it? No one would argue that we're not physically present with our readers when they sit down to read our book. We can't call out to them, "Did you read what I said there on page 114? What did you get out of what I wrote in paragraph three?" And we can't offer further help when they get stuck.

Despite our inability to be physically present, is there anything we can do to make certain our readers are, as Emerson says, able to *mine* what we have offered? The answer, as you undoubtedly surmised by now, is yes.

Before I get too far into this, I want to say that this issue of responsibility to our readers isn't unique to writing spiritual and personal growth books. However, because spiritual writing can be so personal, it is way more important here than in composing, let's say, a software manual, where most readers just want to get down to business and be told which keys to hit. That said, let's pursue this a bit since it is such an important skill for us in this present undertaking.

While it's easy to see how we can call to a friend in the next room and confirm whether or not they've heard us, it's not so easy to understand how we'd take that kind of responsibility for a person reading our book 5,000 miles away. But that's one of the tests we must confront when we decide we want to publish. We find that the solution to this particular puzzle isn't in calling to the next room to make sure we've been heard. Rather, we start to solve this particular puzzle by asking some basic questions: Who are our potential readers? What can we count on from them? What do they bring to the books we have written? Are they accessible, that is, like the person we would call to in the next room, are they in a place to hear what we have to say? And what would we like them to get from our book? If we don't answer questions like these, we can be way off the mark in *what* we choose to say, *how* we say it, and to *whom* we address our words. Let's look at an example.

Early in my writing career, I wrote a book on intuition. All my life I'd heard arguments about how intuition was or wasn't valid. When I sat down to write the book, the tack I decided to take was that I'd try to convince the skeptics of the world that intuitive knowing was valid. While the publisher accepted the book, the book's sales were disappointing. When I read what I'd written, several years later, I instantly recognized where I'd gone wrong. I hadn't known who my potential readers were. The simple fact is that skeptics and doubters rarely walk into bookstores to find something to read that will convince them they should examine their own thinking with the purpose of changing their minds. In short, the readers I addressed simply were not in a place to hear what I had to say. But that wasn't the worst of it. The readers who did look at my book for help developing their intuition found it oddly perplexing. I can imagine them asking,

"Why is this author putting so much energy into convincing me of something I already thoroughly believe and trust?" The readers I had chosen—the skeptics—simply were not in the position to hear what I had to say. And the readers who were in a place to hear were perplexed by my apparent need to sell them on ideas they had no problems with at all.

This was an important lesson for me. Had I thought about it ahead of time, from the perspective I now have about why people read books, I never would have spent a single word on trying to sell my readers on the value of intuition. My core readers were not skeptics but people who themselves already knew about intuition and wanted to learn more. They wanted to hang out with a kindred spirit and perhaps learn about some specific tools for making better use of their intuitive gifts. I wasn't even getting to first base with my core readers because I hadn't even taken the time to identify who they were. How easy it would have been to speak directly to them, knowing from the start that they were completely open to my ideas. They needed no *selling*.

That same year was a time of accelerated learning for me around this issue of knowing my readers and knowing how to reach the readers whose minds would be wide open to what I might have to offer. Soon after my book on intuition was published, I was hired by a well-known lecturer, author, and spiritual teacher. He wanted my help on a series of books he was writing for one of the large New York publishing houses. Because of his teaching schedule he mostly needed someone to do the editing and rewriting his publisher requested. When I read the first manuscript he sent to me, I thought to myself, "I see what the problem is here. These ideas are too basic for readers in this genre. It needs to be more expansive." When I spoke with the publisher in New York, she agreed that this might be the case. I rewrote the first chapter according to my own judgment of what the reader required and sent it back to my client. When he called a few days later, I was certain he was going to praise me for my work. That wasn't to be. The first words out of his mouth were, "Hal, we need to talk. I've got a problem with what you've done here."

I couldn't believe my ears. Hadn't I improved the rough manuscript he'd sent me? Wasn't it much more sophisticated and erudite? Clearly, it was. But as it turned out, that was the problem, not the solution.

"I think I understand what's happened," my client explained, kindly but firmly. "You've rewritten my work for readers who've already done a fair amount of reading and studying, and probably some of their own inner work."

"Yes," I agreed, "that's right." I was still puzzled by what he was trying to tell me.

"But those aren't my readers," he said. "I know my readers pretty well. They're people who are new to spirituality and inner work. They're beginners. They're a little frightened. They don't want things to get too complicated. And maybe they're feeling this stuff is a little in conflict with what their church taught them in Sunday school."

The moment he explained this, I knew that he was way ahead of me in knowing his readers. He knew exactly who was able to hear what he had to say. I must confess, however, that I didn't agree with him right away. It took me about a week to get over myself and take in what he said. In the long run, it was an important lesson for me, one that I have carried with me ever since. My client knew his readers much better than I did, that's for certain. *And he took responsibility for them*, making certain that what he said, and how he said it, reached them. By critiquing my rewrites carefully, and seeing I was off the mark, he acknowledged his readers in a very loving way. He understood their needs and he carefully considered them with every word he spoke or put down on paper. His mission was not to speak to everyone, and not necessarily to those who were already committed to a path of spiritual growth, but to those who were making their first steps into this realm. He knew them. He knew they needed his support and understanding and that this had to come across in the writing. He was aware that he knew more than his readers did about his subject, and that's why they sought him out.

When I tell this story in workshops, there's invariably someone who asks, "Is it right to put ourselves above our readers like that, to assume that we know better than they? Isn't this author being rather egotistical?"

In fact, rather than being egotistical, he's doing just the opposite. He is taking time to ask questions about his readers, to find out how they are different from him and how they are alike.

From his lectures and workshops, he knew people came to him for knowledge that he had and they wanted. Being aware that they looked to him for certain kinds of guidance, he took that responsibility seriously and did his best to deliver. He understood his mission much better than I.

I worked with this author on many different projects over the next several years and learned a great deal from him. What I learned was that responsibility for our readers begins with taking the time to get to know who they are and figuring out how we can best serve them. We assess what we have to offer and who would be most likely to find our offerings most useful. We have to take the time to understand not only what they want from us but what they bring to the books we would write in terms of their attentiveness and their readiness to hear.

"I Only Write for Myself. . . ."

Several times a year I meet writers who tell me that they are working on a spiritual book, but when I ask them who they feel their reader is, they answer, "I just write for myself." If that's really so, this writer is still in the gathering and gestating stage and not quite ready to write a book. It's not until we can fully appreciate the fact that there are readers who want to learn from us that we are able to see the unique problems of writing a book. It's a little like establishing a loving relationship; to love, we need to be able to see "the other" as being different from us, with a unique way of experiencing the world and with dreams and fears that are quite separate from ours. Just as with love, to write a book we need to respect the other's individuality and be able to see him or her as quite different from us. This can include appreciation for how we are alike as well as how we are unalike.

Part of most spiritual teaching has to do with recognizing our oneness and training ourselves not to be run by our egos. When we assume our most effective role as authors, however, we need to take a position that can sometimes seem to contradict those teachings. At least in the area we are writing about, we have to be able to acknowledge that there are readers who might wish to learn from us, and that we may be able to offer something of benefit to others. Don't let false modesty blind you to the fact that there are real readers out there, with hearts, souls, and intellects that long to be fed. Be modest but don't understand your role as an author too quickly.

This respect for the difference between you and your readers is the very essence of accepting a commitment to your readers to share with them who you are and what you have to give. Don't dodge your *author*-ity. Think about your own needs when you sit down to read a book on a subject that's relatively new to you. Don't you want the author you're reading to know more than you? You want them to be your scout in the wilderness, offering at least some assurance that because they've been there before you they can save you some grief, assure you it's safe to venture into this territory, and inspire you.

There are certainly times when you want to read a book less

for information that's brand-new for you than for support and affirmation of beliefs and experiences you share with an author. Sometimes, too, it helps to read a book that clearly articulates an awareness that you find difficult to put into words. Feeling assured that a writer knows what he or she is talking about, and that he or she can speak with some authority about a subject we don't feel confident about, can certainly be useful as well.

If you know you are writing for readers who may already be quite knowledgeable about your subject, you'd better make sure you acknowledge what they know. Don't be afraid to use phrases such as: "You may recall that whenever you've experienced moments of real clarity . . . " or "However familiar you may be with spiritual breakthroughs, if you are like me you probably..." In these subtle ways you let readers know that you appreciate what they bring to whatever you are saying. This, too, is taking responsibility for the relationship you have with your readers.

People on a spiritual path are constantly encountering change in their lives. Change and spiritual growth go hand in hand. Being human, we all tend to resist that part of the process. As Gerald Jampolsky and Diane Cirincione point out in their book *Change Your Mind, Change Your Life*, "There is a part of each one of us that resists change, even change that promises to make our lives better. . . . But by focusing our attention with many daily reminders that tell us there really is another way of looking at the world, we find peace rather than conflict and see that we really do have a choice."[2] Sometimes, we read books for nothing more than these *daily reminders* guiding us through a chosen change. If you're the author of such a book, the contract with your reader is to mark the route through whatever transformation the reader is going through.

It is interesting to me that the responsibility writers are asked to take for their relationship with their readers is itself an important spiritual lesson. As I reflect on this, I cannot help but recall the work of the existential theologians, such as Paul Tillich, Jacques Maritan, and Martin Buber. Their dialogue focused much attention on how important it is to be recognized as *persons*, not simply as *individuals*, and to accept one another fully in our humanness. To relate to one another in all our personhood, with all our strengths and weaknesses, is itself a great undertaking and a great accomplishment. Out of it can come, for both author and reader of the spiritual book, a sense of being accepted and complete, unjudged and at one with all.

Perhaps the greatest lesson any of us has to teach as an author is to touch our readers in such a way that they can remember their spiritual identity, and we do that as much by the relationship we establish with them as by anything we say about a particular subject. Put simply, the quality of the relationship we establish with our readers may well be our greatest message. This begins with taking the time to differentiate the reader from ourselves, respecting the spiritual identity of ourselves and the other person. Only then do we fully grasp the power of this relationship, with each of us bringing ourselves to the page. Accomplishing this is not an easy task, of course, but underlying all spiritual writing, as a kind of subtext, is the question of how far we are willing to go toward fulfilling the implied contract we have with our readers.

The use of language, by its very nature, implies a relationship between at least two people. Were each of us living in complete isolation, there would be no reason for complex language since we would only have need for our own private system of symbols, imagery, and actions that would organize our daily lives and our thought processes. Language revolves around our interactions as complex social beings and our shared desire to relay complex information from one person to another, to teach and learn, and to share our life experiences. When language is working well, as one would hope it might in spiritual writing, it is not just the words we put down on the paper that matter but the quality of the interchange between our readers and ourselves. Reader and writer create together. They come to new understandings together, but this only occurs when the author of a book or article acknowledges his or her reader's presence. This, in itself, is the spiritual lesson that we grapple to learn as authors of spiritual books, and it also happens to be one the most essential teachings of all great spiritual disciplines.

Chapter Three

Know Your Mission

> *It is not the goal but the ultimate mission that kindles the imagination. . . .*
>
> —Charles A. Garfield, Ph.D., and Hal Zina Bennett, *Peak Performance*

Why do we write? What is the passion that drives us to fill pages in our journals or to write what we hope will become a successfully published book? I ask this not out of philosophical curiosity, but because clarity about why you write—your mission—will help you organize and focus your book. By being clear about your mission, you can literally create an inner compass to keep yourself focused and on course as you are writing. This will not only make the writing easier and more fun, it will result in a finished manuscript that says exactly what you want to say.

The ability to focus and stay on course is one of the first things publishers and literary agents look for when considering a new writer's submissions. Good publishers know the importance of the author's mission, for it shows up on every page, keeping readers' interest levels high. They know that there's a relationship between high interest levels and good sales of a book. It's not an ad, a good book review, or the back-cover copy that will sell your book; it's what's between the covers. If your readers are pleased by what you've written, they'll tell others. If they're not, your book goes into the box headed for the used bookstore. There is probably no "product" in the world more dependent on word-of-mouth sales than a book. The subject matter is, of course, important, but no matter how interesting the subject matter, your book's success will depend largely on how good you are at holding and directing your reader's attention.

You don't have to take my word for it. Here's a way to test what I'm saying. Recall a conversation you've had in the past where the speaker never quite found his focus. He kept changing subjects, and the more he drifted the more difficult it was for you to track what was being said. You may have found yourself asking, "Why doesn't he just get to the point?!" Or your own mind trailed off into other subjects, or you became hopelessly entangled in the speaker's words, trying to figure out what he was talking about. In time you might have started tuning out the speaker altogether or you literally walked away. Just as we quickly lose our way when we're on the receiving end of an unfocused conversation like that, the same can happen in an unfocused book. We've got to know where we are going, and it's up to the writer to get the reader on target and keep him on target.

Books sell because they focus readers' attention, whether it's on a subject area, as in nonfiction, or on the story or character development, as in a novel. Lest this sound like I'm putting too much emphasis on book sales, stop for a moment and consider this. Good sales mean your work is doing what every author, publisher, and bookseller wants it to do. It's being enjoyed by, and benefiting, many people: first, it benefits the readers who receive your message; second, it benefits you in royalty income and reputation, allowing you to continue to research, write, or teach; third, it benefits booksellers who sell your book in their stores; and fourth, it benefits your publisher, who is able to stay in business and bring more books like yours to the reading public. In the end, good book sales represent an equitable exchange of energy, which reflects universal laws.

Focus Starts Within

All that being said, an author's mission often starts at a deeply personal level. For instance, as she reflected on her own mission toward the end of her life, author May Sarton said, "I have never written a book that was not born out of a question I needed to answer myself."[1] Most of us who write would agree that our writing efforts are, at least initially, motivated by a question we need to answer for ourselves. But if that were our only motivation for writing, there would be no need to ever reach beyond our private journals. When we turn our interest to writing a book, something besides answering a question for ourselves has begun to occur. Consider this: Books were literally invented to disseminate information to large masses of people. Private journals are for talking to ourselves; books are for talking to other people. We write them because we believe we have something valuable to *share with others,* which points the way to our mission.

You'll notice that May Sarton's mission statement is too broad and general to provide much help in focusing a book. We'd have to look at specific books she'd written to explore her mission. Being a complex person, she explored numerous questions. If I were sure you and I had both read a specific book of hers, we could take that as an example and look at how her mission gave that book focus. Lacking that, let's look at the one book we're sure we are both familiar with—the one you are holding in your hands. Let's use it as our common point of reference and ask the question, What was my mission for writing this book?

To answer that, I'd have to go back nearly a decade, when I began to observe that there were increasing numbers of people coming to my writing workshops to find out how to write a spiritual book. Similarly, the number of people going to other writing seminars for that same purpose has grown exponentially. Many of these writers have spoken of feeling *called* upon to write and of living in a time of spiritual emergence, when a great many people are seeking information that can speed and expand this emergence. While I shared these writers' vision, I couldn't at first see what my contribution might be. After all, I am primarily a writing coach, not a spiritual teacher. What soon became clear, however, was that my mission would be less along the lines of writing a spiritual book of my own and would lean more toward writing a book that would guide others through the process of writing theirs. My mission, then, is *to share with other authors what I know about writing and publishing so that they can write successful books for readers interested in spiritual development*

Over the years, I experimented with a number of different ways of identifying one's mission. Most methods seemed too mechanistic, since I discovered early on that an author's mission is not the same as a goal that we might set for career advancement or financial well-being or even for personal development. I could have said that my goal for writing this book was to describe what it takes to write a successful spiritual book. But that is pretty flat, no doubt because it leaves out an essential ingredient. Notice that my mission statement, at the end of the paragraph above, implies a relationship between myself and my readers—to "share with other authors." It also describes a possible outcome—"so that they can write successful books for readers interested in spiritual development." The relationship that I imagine between my readers and me, as well as the relationship between my readers and their potential readers, is key, for it describes actions resulting from the writer-reader relationship in this book.

For the mission statement to work well, you'll need to be able to experience it almost viscerally. To accomplish this, create a scenario in your own mind about how your readers will be affected by your writing, how they will take in what you've written, and how they will then take it out into the world. Recently, I was helping a friend work on the mission statement for her book on "self-talk," the inner monologue we carry on with ourselves. She certainly knew her material well and even had a clear picture of who her core readers would be. But she could not quite get a handle on her mission, until one morning she wrote me the following email: "I've got it. When I woke up this morning, it was clear and strong. I see my work literally changing the way people think about their relationships, at home, at work, everywhere. I can imagine tensions easing between them and other people, and even bringing new comfort with themselves, because I think as they learn to reframe their inner talk, as I'm proposing, their minds will open to possibilities they'd never even dreamed of before."

This author's excitement about how her book would literally carry her material into other people's lives sparked her imagination and her sense of purpose immediately. She was no longer just recording information for her readers; she was bringing a message that would change their lives. Is this too ambitious or too far-fetched to take seriously? You only need to review a few books that have been important to you to understand the truth expressed here. Reading a book, after all, allows us to enter imaginatively into the author's life, and surely we can be changed by that. The change may be large or small, but we are nevertheless changed.

I searched for a way to teach others how to think about their relationship with their readers, and their impact on readers, while making it integral to their mission statement. I wanted a way to help writers imaginatively enter their readers' lives, for doing so would guide the writers back to their mission. Then one day, while browsing in a large bookstore, the answer came to me. It was right there, staring me in the face as I browsed through the aisles of the bookstore. *Browsing.* That word had a particular meaning for me, implying an open-ended sort of searching. In other words, when I browse I don't always know what I'm looking for but I know I want something and am putting myself in a place where I might just find it.

When I got home that night, the idea came to me that writers could use their imaginations to project themselves into the future, at some time after their book had been published. If they visualized their books already being read, and then imagined the impact of the book on their readers, I believed their missions would become clearer. Based on the experience in the bookstore that night, I came up with the following exercise:

Finding Your Mission

Imagine a woman (or a man, if you wish) walking into a bookstore, not exactly knowing what she is looking for but knowing she wants something. She wanders around for twenty minutes or more exploring every section of the store. Nothing is jumping off the shelves for her, but she is almost praying that something will. And then . . . she comes upon your book. (Granted, it may not be written yet, but bear with me here.) It is standing face out on a table at the center of the store. She walks over to it, intrigued by the title and the cover. She picks it up, reads the back-cover copy. Her eyes light up. She's interested, definitely interested. She turns to the table of contents, and as she reads it her pulse quickens. Could this be it? Could this be what she's been looking for? She flips through a few pages, then takes the book over to a chair in the corner and sits down to read parts of it. For the next twenty minutes she reads, becoming increasingly intrigued.

"This is it!" she tells herself. "I can't leave the store without this book."

She hurries to the cash register, pays for the book and rushes home, where she curls up to read for the next two hours.

Now, taking all of this into account, ask yourself what she got out of your book. What interested her so much that she had to buy it right then and there, then rush home to read it? Using your powers of imagination, take a moment to put yourself in this reader's skin. Imagine being her, reading your book from start to finish. (Don't worry if you haven't written it yet. This is just an exercise.) Imagine sitting down in a quiet place to have a conversation with this reader, who is now a fan of your writing. Ask her questions such as the following:

- What initially enticed you to buy my book? (Have her explain in detail.)

- What's the main thing you got from my book that you will apply in your life?

- What would you like other people to know about my book?

- In fifty words or less, how would you describe my book to your friends?

Let's see what happens when I apply this exercise to my own book. I can imagine my phantom reader replying to the above questions as follows:

"What initially persuaded me to pick up your book was the title, Writing Spiritual Books. *I've been doing journal writing for several years as part of my spiritual practice and have an idea for a book I'd like to write. After reading the subtitle of your book, the copy on the back of the book, and a few things inside the book, I knew this would help me take the next step to fulfill the dream of writing my own book.*

"What I got from your book was an overview of the whole process of writing and publishing a spiritual book, with descriptions of specific skills to help me do it and insider information that I've never seen anywhere else. I've bookmarked all the places that I knew I'd want to come back to when I actually sat down to write.

"Many of my friends do journal writing that is very insightful, and I think they should be sharing it with others. I have told them about your book—mostly that it seems very comprehensive and is almost like having your own private coach to take you through the whole process of writing and getting published.

"Writing Spiritual Books *delivers exactly what the title promises. It describes the ingredients for writing a successful book and teaches the skills I need to do that. It's written in a warm, user-friendly, and supportive style that inspires me, giving me confidence to write the book I dream of writing.*"

This imaginary interview provides you with a process for thinking about how your writing will impact your readers and how they might use the material you're writing. The exercise guides you toward thinking of your writing in terms of a relationship, or contract, that you will be establishing with your readers. It's meant to get you to think of your writing as much more than the reporting of information or telling about your own experiences. You'll still convey information to your readers, and share stories about yourself, but now that information and those stores take place within the context of your interactions with your readers and their interactions with their friends and acquaintances after they've read your book.

After doing this imaginary interview, go through it and highlight the salient points. Then come up with a list of three to five items that your reader found appealing about your book. If readers told you how they would use your material in their own lives, highlight that; it will point you back to your own mission. When you've done this, use the highlighted portions as a reference to write your mission statement of fifty words or less.

If you cannot get your statement down to fifty words or

less, it means that you have not yet identified and focused your mission. The possible causes include:

- **You need to take smaller bites from the material you are working on.** Many first-time authors try to be as comprehensive as possible, putting in enough information to fill an encyclopedia. In writing a popular book, you usually can't go wrong if you err on the side of a narrow, sharp focus. For example, when I first conceived this book, I tried to cover the whole subject of nonfiction writing. The book would have had to be much longer than it presently is. In addition, a person looking for information about nonfiction nature writing would have been turned off by the fact that he had to buy a book about several other genres to learn about the single genre that interested him. I therefore focused my attention on the category that interested me the most, which was writing spiritual books. The remedy, if you're taking on too much, is to narrow down the subject so that the reader's attention will be more focused.

- **You need clarity about what you want the reader to get out of the book.** This is frequently the reason an author has trouble with stating her mission. We often write because we have a personal interest in a certain subject. Our writing may be a way for us to explore that subject, which can be exciting for the writer. But if you are unclear about *what you want your reader to get out of it,* the simple fact is that the reader won't get anything out of it. Your remedy is to ask yourself the obvious question: Who are my readers and what will they do with what I offer them in my book?

- **Your unifying concept needs further development.** Sometimes you can take on a broad variety of seemingly disparate subjects if you find a unifying concept that brings them all together. For example, one author chose to write about human evolution, karma, intuition, choice, addiction, relationships, psychology, illusion, power, heart, soul, and trust. Seems like it could have come out like scrambled eggs. However, the author had a single unifying principle that brought everything together. The book? *The Seat of the Soul*, by Gary Zukav. It was an all-time bestseller on the spiritual books lists and one of Oprah's favorites. If you are juggling what seems like a huge collection of ideas and concepts, the remedy is to look for the single idea that can tie it all together, just as Gary Zukav did. He saw that talking about the "soul" was the umbrella under which all of those issues would fit.

- **You need to do further research or study.** Sometimes the mission is unclear for the simple reason that you need to expand your knowledge of your material. What happens when you're short of knowledge is that holes begin to show up. You find yourself at a loss for what to write. The remedy is to do your further study or research and get a bigger, more complete picture of your subject matter.

You need to clarify who you are talking to—i.e., identify your reader. When I first began writing professionally, thirty-plus years ago, I made the mistake of assuming that my readers were people pretty much like me. They had about the same interests, the same education, approximately the same values. Then an editor complained, "Your writing drifts. It's as though you are daydreaming, talking to yourself." I half-jokingly told him I often did feel I was talking to myself. He laughed and told me, "That's the problem. If your readers were exactly like you, they would have no reason to read the book, now would they?" And he was right, of course. If they were carbon copies of me, my words were only be mirroring what they already knew.

You can, of course, write a book whose purpose it is to affirm your reader's beliefs and values, that is, to say, yes, I believe these things, too. And yet, even when we're looking for confirmation of our own beliefs, we nearly always read in order to expand our horizons. We tend to choose books by authors who are *something* like ourselves, but we also want to feel that the experience of reading will change us in some way, even if it is only to feel more confident about something we already know.

Make sure you know whom you are talking to. Challenge yourself by imagining that your reader doesn't know as much as you know, or consider the possibility that your book is your reader's first introduction to the subject you're writing about.

Assume that you have been called to be this person's

teacher and that she is grateful for what you have brought into her life through your writings. The most exciting nonfiction writing, and therefore reading, comes when you imagine yourself telling a person something she didn't already know.

When you fully grasp the fact that there are real readers out there, people who have lives quite different from yours but who are interested in what you have to say, your writing takes on a new life. There's a deeper connection with your readers. As a result, your sense of mission becomes even more clearly focused.

You Can't Be All Things to All People

With this deepening connection with your reader, you'll begin to discover that you are not writing your book for the whole wide world but for a fairly select group—and that's a good thing. No book ever published spoke to everyone, not even the Bible. There are certainly books with broad, universal themes, such as you might find in great world literature. Yet, even those with the furthest-reaching themes still only speak to a relatively small portion of the reading public. Every time I announce this in workshops, people bristle. We like to think that what we have to say is important to the whole world. And it very well might be! However, don't confuse having a worthwhile message with having a book that will reach everyone.

Publishers and experienced authors talk about having a

community of readers, that is, a group of readers that seek out that author's books because they like what she has to say. But how do we accurately identify a writer's community when her book hasn't yet been published? We can't do that very accurately, but we can at least speculate by looking at the author's mission statement. For example, because of the content of the book you are now holding in your hand, and what I've described in the mission statement, we can speculate that most of my readers will be:

- People who are on a spiritual path
- People who have some writing experience
- People who are interested in writing books on spiritual subjects
- People who know they have a spiritual book in them and are beginning to explore what that might require of them.

If you think about it, that's a pretty specific group of readers—and since you are reading this book, you can count yourself as a member of this community. But let's say that you are planning to write a different kind of book; let's say it's one in which you are going to talk about the ways that sharing a spiritual practice can enhance a relationship. In that case, your community of readers would be different from mine. Your community might include:

- People who are on a spiritual path and who are presently in a relationship
- People who are in relationships where the partners share a spiritual practice or belief system and they want to enhance the spiritual aspects of their relationship
- People in a relationship in which they wish their partner could share their spiritual beliefs and practices
- People looking for relationships that would include a strong spiritual component

Your community of readers and mine might be slightly different. While we'd both draw people from the spiritual community, yours would not need to have an interest in writing, and mine would not need to have an interest in bringing spiritual values into their relationships. Certainly there will be crossover between your community of readers and mine, but where our respective readers will be focusing their attention will be different. As you are writing, think about the unique aspects of your community and use your knowledge of your community to make choices about what you'll write. Don't let your focus drift far from what will interest your community. Always be considering ways to serve that community, to deliver the promise that you've defined in your mission statement.

As writers, it would be nice to think that our readers would be interested in anything we might have to say. But if the gems of wisdom we offer don't serve the focus we've established in our writing, our readers will lose patience and start looking for some other way to spend their time.

I'm coming to believe that the main purpose for books is to help readers focus their attention. In our busy lives, as we're surrounded by nearly unlimited choices and distractions, books become tools for giving our attention to improving a relationship, or to seeking a deeper understanding of our life purpose, or to, well, writing a book. Immersed in a book, we shut off the world around us and focus on an area of our lives we want to improve. Or maybe we sink into the imaginary world of a novel, where we interact with characters whose lives may be very different from our own. As readers we delight in the mental focus good writing provides. Life becomes more manageable when we have a good book to read. Particularly with spiritual books, it's the focus and lessons of a good book that enable us to make new and better choices in our lives, and even to recreate ourselves.

Clarifying our mission isn't just another exercise to fill the pages of a book on writing. Much more than that, it honors this important role that books can perform in our lives, to help us focus our attention for the purpose of deepening understanding and supporting positive change—and hopefully carrying us to transcendent spaces of delight and personal breakthrough.

Chapter Four

Find Models to Follow

> *True originality consists not in a new manner but in a new vision.*
>
> —Edith Wharton, *The Writing of Fiction*

Some years ago I was attending a writers' conference when I came to a booth where a young woman was signing her newly published book. She looked vaguely familiar. Thinking we might have met at a previous book conference, or perhaps at one of my own seminars, I became curious about what she had written. I stopped and picked up her book. While I searched for some way to gracefully introduce myself, she glanced at my name badge, literally screeched my name, and practically upset her piles of books as she clamored around the table to give me a hug. Grabbing one of her books, she scrawled a personal note to me, signed it, and thrust it into my hands, exclaiming how grateful she was to me. Without me, she said, she never could have finished writing her book.

I was incredulous and a little embarrassed. How could I have had such a powerful influence on her if I couldn't recall exactly where we'd previously met? I didn't even know her name! I continued to search my memory but simply could not place her. At last, seeing my confusion and taking pity on me, she explained:

"Do you remember, about five years ago, you were giving a presentation at Transitions Bookplace in Chicago? I was there visiting and came by to hear you talk. You signed a book for me and I told you about my own writing."

I had to confess that I didn't exactly remember. Being on a book tour at the time, I'd met hundreds of people. After awhile, names and faces had become a blur. She filled me in on more details, explaining that she and her partner had a healing center where they taught people how to develop their intuitive abilities. They showed their students how to access spirit guides and use them in healing. Slowly, I began putting it all together.

"Your book on spirit guides was so important to me," she continued. "Naturally, when I sat down to write my book on the subject, I copied yours. It guided me all the way through."

At first I didn't know quite what to say. Had she shamelessly copied my book? And, if she had, why was she not only confessing this to me but celebrating the fact and sharing this information with me so enthusiastically? Most people would be trying to hide the fact. We talked for several minutes, until other people began gathering at her booth wanting copies of her book. We said good-bye and I went on my way.

When I got back to my hotel that night I sat down and read through her book. As it turned out, she hadn't really copied me.

In fact, I wasn't sure why she'd said that. As near as I could tell, she had just used my book as a kind of template. It had given her a model to follow, the way some word-processing programs offer templates for business and personal letters. She had seen that there was a progression in my chapters, from a first chapter that introduced how spirit guides might be employed in everyday life to chapters on how to develop spirit guides through a creative visualization process. But the main body of her material was original, drawn from her own classes and her own work as an intuitive reader. And certainly it was written in a style significantly different from my own.

The more I read what she had to say, the more I could see how different our books really were. I had a difficult time understanding exactly how she'd made use of my book since she had a unique style of writing as well as a unique way of working with spirit guides. She might have started out using my book as a template, but once underway, it appeared, she had created something that was unmistakably her own. If my book was in there, it was as invisible as a proverbial skeleton hidden beneath the flesh.

This encounter would turn out to be a valuable lesson for me, one I've shared with other people in my seminars, and that I am happy to share with you now in this book. Having models to follow, as this author did, is an excellent way to begin. And, no, it's not considered copying.

Different Strokes . . .

When we sit down to write our first book, most of us barely know where to start. There are seemingly infinite ways to organize our work, and many styles of writing. Are we going to approach our subject like an academic, cross-referencing what we write with footnotes to other authors? Are we going to write it like a memoir, keeping the book focused on events that occurred in our own life? And what about self-help formats? For example, there are workbooks with fill-in blanks and assignments for readers to do. There are more open narrative forms, with experiential exercises for readers. There are books that merely talk *about* the subject, with no exercises to do but with stories and anecdotes that allow readers to identify with the author, or with people she talks about in the book. Then there are novels and anthologies. There's even poetry and drama. Choosing a format is important, of course, for if you don't know how to organize your book, you're going to end up with a confusing mess.

Find a Hero

Once you have an idea about what you want to write and who your readership is going to be, search your library for books that can serve as models for you. You're probably going to discover that you already have some favorites. Take a serious look at these and pick out the parts that you think might inspire and guide you. Maybe it's in the way the book is organized, or the way the author writes in short sentences, or the clear and logical steps that are presented. Maybe it's in the stories the author tells to make important points, or something as simple as the lengths of the chapters. Note what you like and experiment with it in your own writing. If it fits you, don't hesitate to make use of it.

Each of us has a preferred way of taking in and communicating information. For example, when I look for books on a new subject I want to learn, I search out self-help books with examples and anecdotes drawn from real life. If it's a spiritual subject, I might also look for novels or memoirs written by or about people who know the territory that I'm just entering. Their example emboldens me to go where I have not gone before.

Here are nine key categories with short descriptions of their characteristics. I've also cited titles of books so you can look them up for yourself.

Anthology: This is a collection of other authors' writings that might include essays, fiction, extracts from larger works, or poetry. I'd include in this category the so-called "book of days," which might be organized with readings for each day of the year. The best anthologies are focused on a specific spiritual theme: for example, forgiveness, the transcendent experience, relationships and spiritual development. Some examples are *Spiritual Literacy: Reading the Sacred in Everyday Life*, edited by Frederic and Mary Ann Brussat, published by Touchstone Books, 1998; *Earth Prayers from Around the World: 365 Prayers, Poems, and Invocations for*

Honoring the Earth, edited by Elizabeth Roberts and Elias Amidon, published by Harper San Francisco, 1991.

Biography: Most of us know of, or have even studied with, spiritual teachers who have been extraordinary influences in people's lives. If you are convinced that they would be of interest to at least 20,000 readers, consider writing a biography about them. There are some spiritual biographies that have been very popular and that have come to hold a special place in the minds of people on a spiritual path. Two excellent examples that come to mind are *Fools Crow: Wisdom and Power*, by Thomas E. Mails, published by Bison Books in 1963, and *Rumi: A Spiritual Biography*, by Leslie Wines, published by National Book Network in 2001. If you want to write spiritual biographies, keep in mind that: the subject must be well known and have lived an interesting life; you will need to be an avid researcher; and, while biographies in general are popular, publishers are going to want lots of evidence that your subject will be of interest to a large enough readership to make publishing the book financially worthwhile for them.

Fiction: In this category, I'd include novels and collections of short stories. In recent years, spiritual fiction has been referred to as "visionary fiction," a term that many bookstores use to distinguish it from literary fiction or the various genre groupings, such as mysteries, science fiction, etc. In recent years, most of us have at least heard about, if not read, *The Celestine Prophecy* by James

Redfield. This was originally a self-published novel that became a bestseller and was picked up by Warner Books, a major New York publisher, in 1994. At about the same time, Marlo Morgan self-published a visionary novel titled *Mutant Message Down Under*, which ultimately sold in the hundreds of thousands. In 1995, it was picked up and published by Perennial Books. Originally, it was viewed as a biography, but today it is mostly regarded as a work of fiction. Certainly, it includes many elements we've come to view as hallmarks of fiction: well-drawn characters, a good story, a bit of suspense, and physical descriptions that take us deep into the world of the story. Dan Millman's *Way of the Peaceful Warrior*, published by H.J. Kramer, still holds up as one of the more popular works of visionary fiction.

Memoir: In the spiritual/New Age market, there has been a great deal of experimentation with this format. According to *Webster's Encyclopedic Dictionary* (1989), memoir is defined as autobiographical writing about a certain period of history. For example, as a boy growing up in Michigan I once read a book about what it was like living in the Upper Peninsula of Michigan before cars, phones, or electricity. The book was written by a woman my great-grandmother's age, who had actually lived through that period. However, there have been books such as *The Invitation*, by Oriah Mountain Dreamer, published by Harper San Francisco in 1999, which uses a variation of the memoir to reflect on events in her own life that led to her spiritual development. Similarly, *Tuesdays with Morrie: An Old Man, a Young Man, and Life's Greatest*

Lesson, by Mitch Albom, published by Doubleday in 1997, relates life teachings the author experienced when visiting a dying friend, Morrie. And finally, there's *Embraced by the Light*, by Betty J. Eadie, published by Gold Leaf Press in 1992.

There's a fine line separating memoirs of this kind, autobiographies, and books written in the next category, Personal Development. That line is increasingly blurred as authors bring together spiritual information and stories about how their own development has been impacted by the material they're presenting in the book. Memoirs can be difficult to sell to a publisher unless they meet certain criteria, such as: they are written by a celebrity that people are fascinated by; they are focused on an important historical event; they reveal little-known information about the philosophies of a specific ethnic group or individual, such as Celtic or ancient Native American teachings; or they show something new about a life passage, such as we find in *Tuesdays with Morrie* and *Embraced by the Light*.

Personal Development: You may notice that I've created two categories that are very similar—personal development and self-help. The main distinction I make between these two is that self-help books contain experiential exercises while personal development books don't. Some leading books written in the personal development format for spiritual readers are *The Power of Now: A Guide to Spiritual Enlightenment*, by Eckhart Tolle, published by New World Library in 1999, and *Soul Mates: Honoring the Mysteries of Love and Relationship*, by Thomas Moore, published by Harper

Collins in 1994. I would add to that *The Seat of the Soul,* by Gary Zukav, published by Fireside Books in 1990 and still a bestseller. In most personal development books, you'll find plenty of anecdotes, personal disclosure on the part of the author, and stories that trace a process of change closely enough that readers could duplicate it in their own lives. But you would generally not come across step-by-step instructions, as you might in a self-help book. My intention is not to create a hard, fast rule here but rather to point out distinctions that are not always clear.

Scholarly: If you've got a scholarly bent—that is, if you love exploring historical roots, literary references, and the studies of other scholars and then documenting what you come up with—you may find great rewards with this form. Some of the classics in this genre are *The World's Religions,* by Huston Smith, published by Harper Collins in 1991, and *The Hero with a Thousand Faces,* by Joseph Campbell, published by Princeton/Bollingen in 1978. Another popular scholarly book, which deals with many spiritual concepts (though it's not advertised as a spiritual book), is *Free Play: Improvisation in Life and Art,* by Stephen Nachmanovitch, published by Tarcher/Putnam in 1990. Many spiritual books blend scholarly text and personal development themes. For example, Rupert Sheldrake's books generally bring scientific studies to bear on spiritual and psychospiritual topics. Take a look at Sheldrake's *The Presence of the Past: Morphic Resonance & the Habits of Nature,* published by Vintage Books in 1989.

Self-help: Self-help books can feature many of the same characteristics that you'd find in personal growth books and scholarly books, but they also incorporate exercises that will help readers take the information in on a direct, experiential level. For example, a reader might find step-by-step instructions for a meditation technique, or for a visualization process, or for any number of things he or she might do to experience firsthand the material the author is presenting. I particularly recommend this approach when you are working with subjects that cannot be adequately presented conceptually—and that would certainly include many spiritual principles.

One of the challenges of the self-help format is that you must write instructions and exercises so that they are readable and not merely distractions for people who don't want to follow your instructions. For that reason, in this book I've included advice on how to write self-help exercises that are truly engaging; see chapter seven, "Exercises That Grab Your Readers' Attention."

Here are some spiritual self-help titles you might want to look over: *The Last Ghost Dance: A Guide for Earth Mages,* by Brooke Medicine Eagle, published by Ballantine Books in 2000; *Soulcraft: Crossing into the Mysteries of Nature and Psyche,* by Bill Plotkin, published by New World Library in 1999; *The Little Book of Letting Go,* by Hugh Prather, published by Conari Press in 2000; and *Forgiveness: The Greatest Healer of All,* by Gerald G. Jampolsky, M.D., published by Beyond Words Publishing in 1999. And don't forget that the book you hold in your hands is an example of the self-help genre.

Workbooks: Like the self-help format, workbooks contain exercises for the reader to do. The big difference is that workbooks usually contain blanks to fill in, encouraging the reader to write or draw in the book. Many publishers avoid this format because it pretty much guarantees that they won't be able to sell copies to libraries. Remember what the librarian told you when your teacher took you for your first tour of the library: "Never, ever write in a book!" For an example of a zany, fun, and informative use of this format, take a look at *Spiritual Doodles & Mental Leapfrogs: A Playbook for Unleashing Spiritual Self-Expression*, by Katherine Q. Revoir, published by Red Wheel/Weiser in 2002. It's absolutely the most innovative use of the workbook I've ever seen, with a strong spiritual theme. If you're seriously considering the workbook format, don't miss this one.

Channeled Books

This category calls for special treatment for two reasons: first, because it entails an explanation for those readers who are not familiar with it but who may find it interesting, and second, because publishing channeled books requires considerations that the other categories don't.

The tradition of "channeling" has probably been around for as long as language itself. In ancient times, long before books, people sat around campfires or in sacred sites exchanging stories and entertaining one another. We know from storytelling traditions that still exist among indigenous peoples that the storyteller often took on the identity of a spirit or perhaps a legendary figure or even an animal and, through assuming the character of the spirit, figure, or animal, disclosed the wisdom of that being. Sometimes what the storyteller revealed was far beyond his or her own knowledge, leading listeners to believe that human consciousness was not limited by the boundaries of the physical body. The famous psychoanalyst C.G. Jung proposed the idea of a collective consciousness, which we all can access during certain moments of our lives and which some people can access at will. When linked with this consciousness, we are able to tap into a source of knowledge quite beyond our everyday awareness.

Dr. Jung, for example, tells of a character he called Philemon, who would certainly qualify as a channeled entity in today's world. Jung writes that Philemon "and other figures of my fantasies brought home to me the crucial insight that there are things in the psyche which I do not produce, but which produce themselves and have their own life. Philemon represented a force which was not myself."[1] He speaks of having conversations with this being and learning of things that he had never previously studied or even thought about. Philemon represented superior insight to Jung, though Philemon continued to be a mysterious figure—as real to Jung as any other person he knew, though only available to him through his inner world.

In modern times, meaning the past 100 years or so, channeling has been popularized by people like Edgar Cayce, who channeled health readings in a hypnotic state, and Robert

Hoffman, a businessman who channeled a systematic therapeutic approach known as the "Hoffman Quadrinity" process through the spirit Dr. Siegfried Fischer. There was Jane Roberts, who channeled Seth, whose work on creativity and personal transformation still ranks high on the list of must-read books for people on spiritual paths. And then there is *A Course in Miracles*, spiritual teachings channeled by Dr. Helen Schucman, an academic psychologist.

Channeled books seem to go through periods of popularity every twenty years or so. While larger publishers tend to steer away from them and be very skeptical of their validity, good ones—that is, channeled books with solid messages—are still sought out by thousands of readers. At the time of this writing, most channeled books are published either by their authors or by small, independent publishers who specialize in metaphysical and occult works.

Anytime I bring up the subject of channeling during lectures or workshops, people invariably ask if I think it is "real." The best way I can answer that question is to borrow a quote from Dr. Arthur Hastings, the author of what is arguably the most responsible and well-researched book on channeling, *With the Tongues of Men and Angels*. Dr. Hastings states, "Regardless of the validity of the claims of supernatural agency, the fact remains that mentally healthy individuals experience these phenomena. Moreover, a large number of these messages contain meaningful information and exhibit knowledge and talents of which the channeler is completely unaware. Whatever one's view of the origin of the messages, the phenomenon itself merits serious examination."[2]

If you are planning to write a channeled book, and you are adept in the art of channeling, be prepared to self-publish your work or to publish it through a small publisher that specializes in metaphysical books. I've worked with at least two authors whose channeled books were eventually published by small publishers, and both sold moderately well. So I am convinced that if the material is good, regardless of its source, it will find a readership.

Some of the channeled titles you might look at are *A Course in Miracles*, published by the Foundation for Inner Peace in 1975, or any of the Seth books by Jane Roberts, published by New World Library. You might like Ken Carey's books *The Starseed Transmissions* and *Return of the Bird Tribes*, published by Harper San Francisco.

Making Choices

As you peruse these books, or others that are your favorites, you'll probably find that the categories don't always have crisp boundaries. For example, some personal development, scholarly, and self-help books may seem to be a blending of all three genres. Certainly, there are many personal development books that quote other authors and authorities, giving them the look of a scholarly book. And scholarly books may contain anecdotes either about the authors themselves or about others whose stories come up in the presentation of the material. So don't worry too much about how neatly your material fits in one or another form. The main thing is to look at which form feels most comfortable for you, given what you wish to write.

How do you make the kinds of choices we're exploring here? Some of these choices will be obvious, of course. Should your main interest be writing a biography, you're probably not going to choose to do it as a workbook. However, how would you choose between self-development and self-help? With the latter format, you're going to be writing exercises and instructions. If you are planning to teach a workshop based on the book, those exercises are going to come in handy. Workshops are generally based on experiential exercises, and by writing a self-help book you'd have a good start. Also, if you are already teaching a seminar with exercises, you may find that the self-help form is quite easy for you.

Ultimately, though, it's a matter of what feels good to you. Try experimenting with different formats, using them as templates, just as my friend did at the beginning of this chapter. Don't be timid about this. Most accomplished authors do it. Some may not do it consciously, but they definitely are influenced by writers whom they've read and liked.

While marketability isn't the only reason to write a spiritual book, I think it's a good idea for those seeking good publishers to know that some formats are easier to sell than others. For example, self-help and self-development books account for the largest number of books sold. Spiritual novels and visionary fiction, however, account for a small percent of total sales across the entire industry. Yes, *The Celestine Prophecy* and *Mutant Message Down Under* were runaway bestsellers a few years back, but since then nobody has come even close to repeating their success.

Finally, if you are teaching seminars or offering coaching, lectures, or counseling, books on personal development can be wonderful calling cards. They let potential students or clients preview what you have to offer, and producing a book adds credibility to whatever you do.

Chapter Five

Mapping Out Your Book

The most beautiful thing we can experience is the mysterious. It is the source of all true art and science.

—Albert Einstein

I'm frequently asked, "Do you outline your books before you sit down to write them?" The answer is yes, but with two significant qualifiers. First, I use what some will view as an unconventional method of outlining. And second, as a book evolves it takes on a life of its own. When that happens, my outline may change. Particularly when writing a spiritual book, we need to allow ourselves to be responsive to what we are creating as we go, and we should be open to changing our plans if that means making the book better.

Most of the spiritual books I've either written or helped others write have gone through several transformations along the way. It seems especially true in this kind of book, for the writing itself can carry you into new areas of discovery and personal growth. When that happens, you may want to rethink parts of what you initially planned to talk about. If you're being honest with your material, this can mean going back to revise the outline. The changes don't usually alter core ideas, but it's best to do outlines with a promise to yourself that you'll not become a slave to the outline itself. Always remember that your main goal is to produce the best book you can, not to prove how well you can adhere to your original plans.

Books are generally regarded as highly linear and structured, so writers tend to assume that a rigid outline is called for. What I mean by this is that you start on page one, read that, turn to the next page, and so on. You follow a simple, straightforward line through the reading or writing of the book. That's linear, and a very left-brain orientation (exacting and set). Language, too, is linear. There are set rules for spelling, constructing sentences, etc., and if you don't know and follow those rules our readers may not be able to understand you. Sentences go together like assembling a train, one segment (or car) after another until they all line up in a nice, coherent row. At least that's how it appears on the surface. However, while you may be working with a form that is primarily linear, when writing a spiritual book you are also working with the human consciousness, which operates not just on cerebral and linear principles but also in the emotional and spiritual realms—and these are nonlinear, right-brain-oriented areas.

When you are writing a spiritual book, you are using a left-brain activity (language) to express material that requires right-brain participation. To do that well, you need tools of communication that are free-flowing and intuitive as well as rational and coherent. And that's where mind mapping can be helpful.

Mind Mapping

Mind mapping (sometimes called "clustering") is a system of note-taking originally developed by Tony Buzan in the 1970s. Over the years, he and others have developed it further for outlining. I first learned about this system while working with Charles Garfield on his book *Peak Performance: Mental Training Techniques of the World's Greatest Athletes.*[1] He employed it in his program for the mental training of professional athletes and Olympians. It was particularly useful for this purpose, since the holographic, or three-dimensional, elements of mind mapping made sense for athletes who were trying to coordinate physical, emotional, and even spiritual faculties to achieve higher levels of performance. In that respect, the writer of spiritual books has a lot in common with the athlete, since both writer and athlete must deal with several layers of reality simultaneously.

Conventional outlining—the kind you learned in high school, using roman numerals, upper and lower case letters, etc.—requires us to put our ideas in order before we've given them much of a chance to develop. While this kind of ordering can provide us with an excellent list of what we might wish to cover, it also tends to make the writing stilted and sterile, putting emphasis on order rather than content. This emphasis leaves little or no room for an open and free flow of ideas.

Mind mapping, by contrast, provides a way to get our thoughts down on paper while implementing a constant feedback loop between the notes recorded on paper and the brain. The graphic nature of mind mapping stimulates the creative process, even suggesting relationships between subjects that we might not otherwise see.

With that as an introduction, let's go on to the instructions.

The ABC's of Mind Mapping

Preparations

In Figure 5.1, you'll find an exemplary mind map I made of this book in the early stages of its development. This will give you a picture of how your own mind mapping might look.

Supplies You'll Need

While you can do mind mapping on a standard sheet of 8 1/2 x 11-inch paper, I recommend that you get a pad of oversized newsprint, 14 x 17 inches or larger. One writer friend keeps a flip chart on an easel in his office and uses it to outline books, chapters, and even paragraphs. Also get at least one medium-point felt-tip marker. If you wish, get markers in several different colors to code different elements of the book. While I don't use col-

RECEPTIVITY & CHANGE
Journals
Personal writing
why pub?
why private?
From Revelation
Publication
Steps & Processes
Online?
Agents
Publishers
Books for going farther
Resource Section
Printers
Web for writers
P.R.
Bookstores
Author
Attention
Mission
Focus
Reader
Inspiration
Fiction?
Howto
Models
Scholarly
Other
Spiritual Writing
Vocab
Language
Tone-Voice
Journaling
Choosing Tools
Writing In Spirit
level of disclosure
Clustering
Experiential
Mind Mapping
John Muir
Exercises
Stream consciousness
Read-ability
Auto Matic Writing ??
compliance or inspiration ?

Figure 5.1

ored markers, many people find the color coding helpful. For example, you might use red ink for noting chapters, blue for subjects that are of high priority but that are not chapter titles, and green for themes that cross over into many different areas of the book.

Be Open and Imaginative

Don't be afraid to invent, experiment, and allow your mind to wander, freely making associations with the different subject areas that come up for you as you go along. When mind mapping is working well, one notation triggers another, and that's good. Think of this work as nonlinear brainstorming.

Relax as you make your notes. You may even find that it's good to spend a few moments in meditation before mind mapping your book. Send your inner critics off to the moon, or some other remote place, for a vacation.

There have been dozens of books written on mind mapping, with each author presenting a slightly different twist. What this indicates to me is that there is no single way to do this. So feel free to develop your own mind mapping system, allowing it to evolve as you familiarize yourself with the basic principles of this system and continue to work with it. Don't treat the system I present here as a last and final word on the subject. Just use it as a model for getting started and then tailor it to your needs.

Brainstorming: Step One

Construct your mind map like a galaxy, with a *sun* at the center and various *planets, satellites,* or *moons* circling around it. The sun at the center represents the mission, or core idea, of your book. For example, in this book the core idea is *spiritual writing.* This is the sun around which everything else will revolve. Notice the circle in the center (Figure 5.1) that I've named "Spiritual Writing."

Start your own map in this way, with a circle in the middle of the page enclosing what you presently believe to be the mission, or core idea, of your book. Not sure what the core idea is yet? Then either write in your best guess or leave it blank for now. As you continue this process, it will reveal itself to you in time.

Brainstorming: Step Two

In the periphery of the sun, start writing down any ideas that come to mind as you think about your core idea. Circle them but do not yet connect them with lines. Keep writing down ideas, freely associating each time you do, putting them in whatever spaces you want. Sometimes only a word or two will come to your mind. At other times short sentences will come. Just write down whatever comes to mind and circle these thoughts with your felt pen.

Some people prefer to use Post-its®, writing ideas on notes

that can be easily moved around on the paper. Once you begin to see the order of things (see following), you can draw the notes in on the paper.

Don't worry if what you begin to see at this part of the process is a clutter of notes.

Brainstorming: Step Three

After you've filled up a page in this way, with a bunch of planets and satellites, start looking for those that you feel make big contributions to the core idea and that might become chapters. For example, I knew from having written other spiritual books that using anecdotes—i.e., telling stories—was an important way to connect with readers. It was clear to me from the start that this was a big enough theme to become a chapter.

After you've picked out some ideas that you feel should be chapters, look over other circled ideas you've noted and see if there are any more that could, with some further development, become chapters.

Each time you pick out a chapter, draw a straight line directly from it to the sun. Each chapter is now like a planet, with a direct connection to the sun, or core idea.

Brainstorming: Step Four

You will probably have some ideas that are still important to you but that don't seem big enough to become chapters. Look around and see if these could be developed in meaningful ways within one or more of the chapters you've tentatively established. For example, in the first outline of this book I noted "anecdotes" as one of the smaller satellites, or moons, of the storytelling chapter. As I developed the work further, I saw that anecdotes would find their way into nearly every chapter, since they can be used for illustrating virtually any topic. While this was true, the main place I'd be talking about anecdotes was going to be the storytelling chapter, so I connected "anecdotes" with the storytelling planet.

When you find chapters where these smaller ideas fit, connect the ideas to those chapters with a line.

Brainstorming: Step Five

Once you've noted chapters and connected the satellites, start reading over what you've done. As you look at the chapters, imagine what you might want to discuss within them. Let your mind roam around within the outline, freely associating. As new ideas or subject areas arise, add these to the mind map, connecting them with the chapter where you feel they belong. You may also discover new chapters that you will want to write.

As you go along, your mind map may become a swirl of chaotic circles and lines. While you've been mapping out the interrelationships of the parts, the drawing itself has gotten harder to read. It is at this point that you'll want to go on to Refining the Map: Step Six.

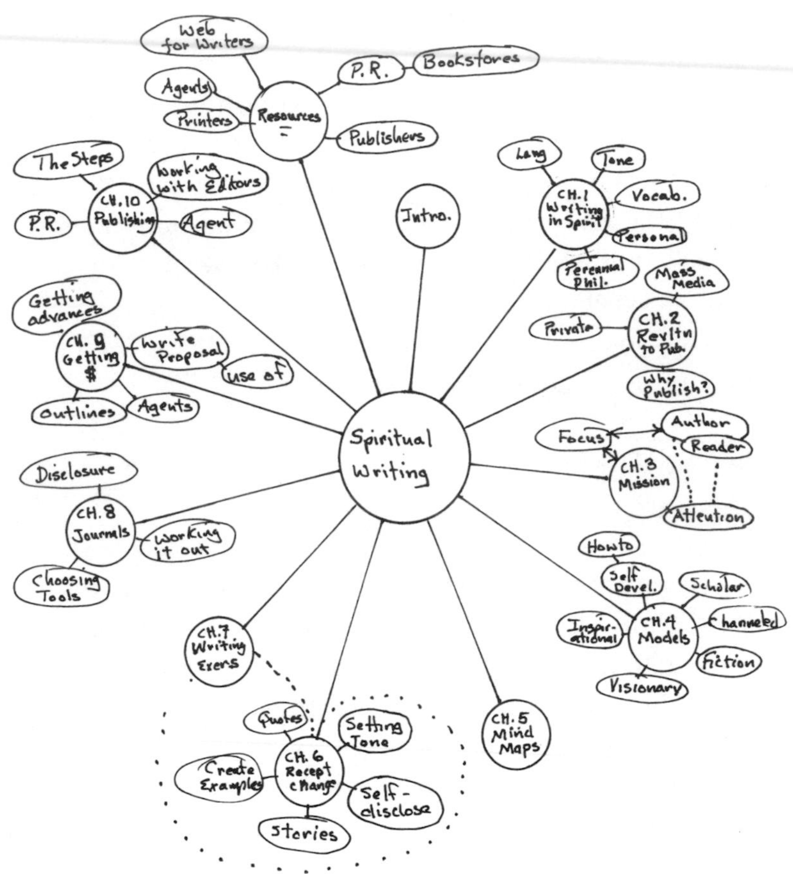
Web for Writers
Agents
Printers
Resources
P.R.
Bookstores
Publishers
The Steps
Working with Editors
CH.10 Publishing
P.R.
Agent
Intro.
Lang
Tone
CH.1 Writing in Spirit
Vocab.
Personal
Perennial Phil.
Mass Media
Private
CH.2 Revltn to Pub.
Why Publish?
Getting advances
CH. 9 Getting $
Write Proposal
use of
Outlines
Agents
Spiritual Writing
Focus
Author
Reader
CH.3 Mission
Attention
Disclosure
CH.8 Journals
Working it out
Choosing Tools
How to
Self Devel.
Scholar
Inspir-ational
CH.4 Models
Channeled
Fiction
Visionary
CH.7 Writing Exers
CH.5 Mind Maps
Quotes
Setting Tone
CH.6 Recept change
Create Examples
Self-disclose
Stories

Figure 5.2

Refining the Map: Step Six

Working from the brainstorming map you've just completed, begin ordering your chapters, from one to whatever number you find. Number them on the brainstorming map and then copy them in clockwise order around the sun, or core idea (Figure 5.2).

Refining the Map: Step Seven

Having drawn the main part of the mind map—the sun and the planets (chapters) surrounding it—start putting in satellites around each chapter. Continue to work in a freewheeling manner, but make the map more orderly now, so that it will be easy for you to read. For example, as you start drawing the satellites describing issues you'll be talking about in chapter one, you might have a sudden insight about something that you should do in chapters six and eight. Go ahead and draw in those ideas around their respective planets.

At this point in the process, you should have a revised mind map that will give you a clear picture of what your book will cover. You may want to adjust the order of the chapters, satellites, or moons. You may want to add chapters. And you will undoubtedly think of new material that you'll want to include in the chapters. Continue to hold onto the freewheeling mindset you've been working with, staying open and receptive so that new ideas can suggest themselves.

I sometimes go through a dozen or more mind maps before arriving at a point where I'm satisfied with what I have. At that point, I move on to write a working chapter outline based on the work I've done with the mind maps.

The Working Chapter Outline

The working chapter outline is generated from the mind maps you've created. It consists of the titles of the chapters and 125 to 250 words describing what you wish to accomplish in each one. I recommend that you write this description in the first person to remind yourself that you are describing not just objective material but a relationship that you are creating between you and your reader. Each chapter description can be as simple as the following:

> **Chapter Five: Mapping Out Your Book**
>
> In this chapter I will discuss the importance of outlining the book in a way that is intuitive and open, employing a freewheeling approach that stimulates creative thought. I'll emphasize that writers should not allow themselves to become slaves to the outline but to look

> upon the outline as a tool that is constantly changing. I will present step-by-step instructions for mind mapping (also called "clustering") the entire book and each chapter. I'll cite Charles Garfield's description of how mind mapping is used by high performance athletes (from his book *Peak Performance: Mental Training Techniques of the World's Greatest Athletes*) and I'll talk about why the same methods are valuable for writers. Next will come a discussion of how to write a good working chapter outline based on the mind map work just completed, closing with a basic but highly workable formula for writing a nonfiction book for today's readers.

You may wish to put in more details as you go along, such as quotes from other writers or anecdotes that come to mind. As with the mind mapping process, stay loose, and if you see changes or additions you want to make, do so. As any professional writer will tell you, "Writing is rewriting." At some point, of course, you will say, "Okay, now I'm done." When that happens, but only when that happens, you stop and do one final rewrite of the chapter outline. You'll find this invaluable not only because it gives you a map to follow as you write the book but also because it will help you write a selling proposal to present to a literary agent or publisher (see chapter nine).

A word of caution here: There's a tendency, even among seasoned authors, to dash off a book outline to get to their agent or publisher. The outline can seem like busy work, keeping us away from the "real writing." If you feel this happening, slow down. Most nonfiction books are sold on the basis of a proposal, which contains this outline. Mediocre, dashed-off outlines kill even the best projects. Publishers need to be able to get a handle on your book ideas, and the outline is how you give them that. I have taken as long as three months developing outlines for some books I've either authored or worked on—to give you a sense of what's a reasonable effort for this undertaking. That's not full-time, naturally, but within those three months I went back and forth many times, adding chapters, cutting others, rearranging the subjects within chapters, and so on.

Formula for Success

While I don't believe in formula writing, I do believe that there are fundamental principles that every writer should take into account when writing a nonfiction book. While not exactly a formula, these principles can help you to develop a solid plan for what your book is going to say. Here are some organizing principles I consider each time I write a nonfiction book:

1. **The Introduction** (no more than eight or ten manuscript pages): Some publishers today argue that nobody reads introductions anymore. They may be right; I'm simply not sure. I do know that I usually read them if they tell me something about the author and what motivated her to write her book.

My recommendation, therefore, is to write an introduction but to limit it to telling your reader what motivated you to write the book. Do not include anything that will be absolutely necessary for readers to know. Focus instead on making a strong, intimate connection with your readers, letting them know that you have a passion for what you are writing and that your goal is to share it with them.

2. **How to Use This Book** (optional; maximum three manuscript pages): Not all books require this. As the title says, this section suggests ways the reader might read the book. I included a "How to Use This Book" segment in this book because I wanted to alert readers to the "Resources" section and to the idea that they do not have to read the chapters in order. For example, a reader may have already written part of his book and may want to know about publishing (chapter ten) before he reads the chapters on writing.

   The first time I ever used this convention was in *The Well Body Book*, which I wrote in the early 1970s. A book on holistic health, it contained a diagnosis and treatment section, written by my coauthor, Mike Samuels, M.D. We had decided that many people would want to know that they could immediately turn to that section for help if they had symptoms they were concerned about. Plan on using a "How to Use This Book" segment whenever you have stand-alone reference material that the reader might wish to turn to immediately.

3. **Chapter One:** I recommend that you approach the first page or two of chapter one with special attention. What you write here should draw your readers in, making them want to read the rest of the book. You want to pique their interest, inspire them, and focus their attention on the subject you'll be covering in the pages ahead.

While I always write a first draft of the first chapter, I do the final rewrites of that chapter after writing all the other chapters. In this way, I am completely familiar with everything contained in the book. My own focus is far clearer at this point than it was when I first sat down to write, and by rewriting the first chapter I can convey a stronger sense of where the book is going. If you do the same, your readers will be grateful for the focus you provide. The chapter will read with an authority and conciseness that you simply could not have provided in the beginning.

Don't be afraid to spend twice as much time rewriting chapter one as you spend rewriting any two other chapters in the book. Remember, if you can get your readers' attention here, there's an excellent chance that you'll have their attention throughout the rest of the book. That attention and focus will make your book a standout, leading your readers to tell others to read it. Many years ago, the editor-in-chief of one of the world's largest publishing houses told me, "Never forget that your book is its own best advertising . . . and that begins on page one, chapter one."

After chapter one, you're on your own. Your own material, your style of writing, your own way of prioritizing your material, will all come into play. The one thing I can recommend, however, is that you should be asking the following questions with every page you write:

- Have I covered everything the reader needs to know up to now?
- What logically follows after this chapter?
- Does what I'm writing in this instant really belong in this chapter or another?
- Does what I'm writing in this instant belong in my next book rather than here?
- Would an anecdote or illustration help to make this point easier for the reader to get?
- How would my reader be feeling right now? Would a supportive word or two help?

Throughout the book, pause from time to time and then put yourself in your readers' position. Read over what you've just written and check in to see how you, the author, have done. The checklist is excellent for this.

Stumped on a chapter? Got writer's block? It happens to the best of us, but don't worry. Nine times out of ten the *cure*, if you will, can be found in going back to mind map just the chapter you're working on. You'll generally find the missing piece or the little dead end that has got you stumped. Making an addition or cutting something will usually get you back on track.

As I put the final touches on any outline, be it for a whole book or a single chapter, I like to remind myself of something said by Plutarch 2,000 years ago: "The mind is not a vessel to be filled but a fire to be ignited." That principle should be in your mind from the initial planning stages of your book through every page you write. If a book is to be successful, reaching the readers you hope to reach, it must, as Plutarch says, ignite fires.

Chapter Six

Fostering Receptivity and Change

As a gypsy storyteller out on the puszta would say as he sets aside his fiddle to gaze into the fire, it's an important story, and the hour is getting late. Let's save it. Next time you come to see me, I'll tell what happened, and we'll play some music.

—Victor Walter, *The Voice of Manush*

Many spiritual insights call upon us to make personal changes, sometimes significant ones. And as we all know, along with the prospect of change comes resistance. As authors of spiritual books we can't ignore the reality that what we are writing may simultaneously trigger both the desire for change and resistance to it. To be effective as authors of these books, we need to foster our readers' receptivity and openness to change, or else our efforts may be wasted. Whatever we write should be offered in a supportive way, helping readers to feel safe as they anticipate taking a new step.

Were we writing a novel, we'd take it for granted that we would be causing our readers to feel joy, fear, suspense, anticipation, love, peace, etc. In writing nonfiction, we may not think we're doing that. But in fact, we are. The "voice" we develop in the book, the way we present the material, the degree of self-disclosure we use, the expectations we put on our readers, and how much direction we give them, all affect how our readers are going to feel. Because we do make an impact on our readers, and because of the nature of the material we work with, we need to ask questions such as, "What kind of emotional and intellectual atmosphere does my writing create in my readers' minds? Am I creating a sense of trust and safety where readers feel secure about concepts that may trigger significant change for them? What can I do through my writing to foster the kind of trust readers need to make full use of the information I am writing about?" The solutions we're seeking in answer to these questions mostly have to do with skills that we can learn, and that's what we'll be doing in this chapter.

Be a Storyteller

The storyteller has much to teach us about creating a trusting atmosphere. Think for a moment about the words "once upon a time," which we associate with oral storytelling conventions. These words have a magical effect on adults and children alike. While writers of spiritual books are rarely going to use those same words, we'd do well to look at what happens when we use a storytelling voice. That voice can open a reader's mind to even the most challenging ideas. To hear how others have approached a challenge similar to the ones we're facing takes some of the pressure off us. Plus, hearing of others trials and victories gives us courage and convinces us that we can prevail.

Stories and anecdotes that tell your readers how the ideas you're presenting have benefited you are particularly important since, if you've done your job well, readers will want to identify with you and may even model your behavior. Telling your own stories sends an important message that you, and presumably others, have been there, done that, and have come out the better for it.

Don't be afraid to share personal stories with your readers, even stories that reveal your human shortcomings. Focused disclosure of this kind can illustrate important points while teaching your readers that you are, after all, only human. If these solutions are accessible to you, they're accessible to your readers as well. Readers need to know you are not superhuman.

Anthropologists tell us that storytelling was the primary way early societies communicated complex ideas. If you are committed to writing engaging as well as instructive and supportive books, keep notes in your personal journal about your own behavior—your resistance to new concepts, for example, and how you lived beyond that resistance. In addition to remembering your own stories, keep on the lookout for other people's stories that can highlight the lessons you are offering your readers.

In a passage from her book *Maps to Ecstasy*, Gabrielle Roth tells her readers what it means to make the distinction between the calculating, linear mind and something larger (that is, the universal mind that experiences the world beyond mere words and calculations). To help illustrate this, she offers the following anecdote from her own life: "When my son was three years old, he astonished me one morning when I overheard him talking to a grown-up friend of ours. This man was completely out of touch with his heart, unable to see anyone but himself. This particular morning he was mindlessly lecturing my small son, who abruptly stopped eating his cereal, stared at this hollow man, and blurted out: 'Words, words, words—is that all you have!'" [1]

There are inherent qualities in storytelling that connect author and reader and that establish a sense of trust, even as these stories function as lively examples of a point you are trying to make. Convinced of the power of storytelling to convey truths not easily revealed with words, one of the authors I worked with sprinkled Sufi parables throughout his book. Each of these stories offered a teaching that helped support the author's message. Most of the parables in this case were of Nasreddin Hodja, a legendary figure in the Muslim faith, whose tales primarily used humor to teach lessons. One in particular was about personal identity: Nasreddin Hodja goes into a bank to cash a check. The teller asks if he can produce proof of his identity, so that she can confirm that he is who he claims to be. Hodja puzzles over this for a moment, then reaches into his pocket, pulls out a small mirror, and peers into it. After carefully contemplating what he sees, he assures the teller, "Yes, that's me!"

Like other parables told about Nasreddin Hodja, this one amuses us even as it points out the absurdity of depending on a piece of paper to confirm who we are. The story not only reveals a certain truth, but it also makes the reading experience enjoyable by providing us with a little chuckle in the process.

Who Said That?

When I first started writing spiritual and personal growth books, a publisher friend of mine told me that readers love memorable quotes that articulate difficult concepts. When you can find a quote that simplifies without trivializing an important point, you're really in luck. In his book *Deep Healing: The Essence of Mind/Body Medicine,* Dr. Emmett E. Miller includes a wonderful American folk saying that's a perfect example of this kind of quote: "Be who you is, cuz if you ain't who you is, you is who you ain't."[2] This states a truth that other writers have spent whole books explaining. Because of its sharp focus, its country dialect, and its economy of words, we are not likely to forget it.

Authors of spiritual books should be avid collectors of quote books relevant to the subject matter they are working with. Such books abound on the reference shelves of used bookstores. At the very least, have *Bartlett's Familiar Quotations,* which is now in at least its twentieth edition. That book has been an author's and lecturer's standard for at least 130 years!

I also recommend *The New Beacon Book of Quotations by*

Women, compiled by Rosalie Maggio. I added this excellent volume to my quote-book collection after I noticed that Bartlett's, and several other quote books I own, focus heavily on male writers. If you follow a specific spiritual discipline, such as Buddhism, Hinduism, Christianity, or Judaism, find books of quotes specific to those traditions.

Walk in Your Readers' Moccasins

Remember that in everything you write your main mission is to make the material you're writing accessible to your readers. The best way to do that is to put yourself in your readers' shoes. As the saying goes, walk a mile in his moccasins. If you have developed a relationship with your ideal reader, as I described in previous chapters, this will be easy for you to do.

I have often turned to Hugh Prather's books for models of very clearly written and highly accessible material, even about very complicated human processes. It's obvious that Prather never asks a reader to do something he hasn't done himself. What's more, his writing shows me that he has given a great deal of thought to his readers. In his book *Notes on How to Live in the World and Still Be Happy*, Prather talks about making decisions to get rid of material possessions that no longer serve us. He suggests that we sit quietly in a room where we are surrounded by objects that we want to assess for any value they still hold for us. He advises us to close our eyes, relax for a moment, and then open our eyes and focus deliberately on the first item that comes to our attention. He then goes on:

> Look calmly at this item and ask yourself the following questions. (You can write out the answers if you wish, but after the first possession or two you may sense that you can be deliberate enough to do this mentally.)
>
> 1. Do I still use this? (As a decoration, a tool, a symbol of certain memories, etc?)
>
> 2. Am I still taking care of this? (Dusting it, servicing it, polishing it, etc.)
>
> 3. If I am neither caring for it nor using it, in what specific ways do I fear letting it go? ("I may use it some day." "I might offend the one who gave it to me." "It's costly and I don't see how I will ever recoup its value.")
>
> If after answering these there is still a question whether to keep this particular possession, close your eyes and project into the future both keeping and not keeping it. Then ask yourself, "Which course of action will add to my present peace?" [3]

Notice how Prather seems to anticipate our experiences and the thoughts and feelings that are likely to come up for us with each step. That's the essence of supportive writing. The effects he manages to project are that: (a) he has done what he's describing or he's experienced it firsthand; (b) he has cared enough about us to relive each step in his own mind so that we can follow it, even if he is not there in person to guide us.

Let's explore this a little further by looking at how this same material might look if it was not written in the way Prather did it. It might go something like this:

Key questions to ask for deciding whether to keep or discard personal objects:

- Is it useful to me?
- Am I taking care of it?
- What scares me about getting rid of it?

Answer these questions and make choices accordingly.

What distinguishes Prather's treatment is his ability to imagine his readers as they are reading his words—to care enough about his readers to take the time to consider what they might be going through when sorting through possessions that once may have meant a great deal to them. Even short explanations, such as those that Prather has enclosed in brackets, can give your readers the feeling that you have had enough concern about them to anticipate their questions and needs. You've walked in their moccasins and projected yourself into future time when your reader will snuggle up before a crackling fire to read your book and encounter what might turn out to be a challenging exercise.

There are, of course, readers who just like to get to the bottom line as quickly as possible. Those few may prefer the second model I present here. But let me assure you that you will gain a lot more readers with the Prather model and the other ideas I've described here. The main reason for this assumption is that spiritual and personal growth readers are not just looking for *raw information*; rather, they are moved by the quality of the relationship you create with your words and by the sense of connection that they experience when they read your books. They feel supported by you and are convinced that you will give them help along the way. You seem able to get right inside their heads, which is something that words can do quite well.

What's in a Voice?

It's not just *what you say* but *how you say it* that carries a message to your readers. Many years ago, when I was still a college student, my car broke down one evening during a trip across the country. I called for towing service at one of those roadside emergency phones seemingly in the middle of nowhere. I was upset, hundreds of miles from home and with very little money for repairs. The wind was blowing and the roar of passing trucks nearly deafened me. When the towing service answered, I was happily surprised to hear the friendly and sympathetic voice of a young woman. I immediately felt relieved and comforted. I told her where I was—standing alongside the busy highway about a quarter-mile from my car—and she answered, "Oh, gosh, it's dangerous out there. I'll radio my husband right away and have him pick you up. He's got another car on his rig, but he's not far away. I'll tell him to take you to Jean's Café on the next off ramp. You can catch your breath there and have a cup of coffee until he can get to your car."

That kind voice was like a message from heaven. Almost immediately, I regained my courage and confidence. Less than ten minutes later, a red tow truck pulled up, driven by the woman's husband, who was as friendly and reassuring as his wife. A few minutes later, he dropped me off at the café and arranged to pick up my car in an hour or so. It turned out that the food at Jean's Café wasn't half bad and there was a small motel right next door, where I was able to spend the night while my car was being repaired.

This kindness of the tow truck driver and his wife is hardly an everyday occurrence, as anyone who has ever had a breakdown on a strange highway can tell you. However, since that evening I've always thought of it as an excellent example of what makes the difference between communication and information. Communication always includes caring about what's going on for the person you are communicating with, just as the tow truck driver and his wife did that evening. Information focuses, instead, on facts, with little or no concern for human factors that may be involved.

Had the exchange between the three of us been strictly informational the night my car broke down, I would have spent a hot, dusty, uncomfortable, and teeth-gritting hour and a half sitting in my car by the side of the road. Writing can be like that: the only thing to differentiate information from communication may be the presence of a friendly, caring voice.

As an author, especially the author of a spiritual book, you want your writing to work for other people, to help them or inspire them in many ways. If you fail to do that, your books are not going to sell. Never forget that books, perhaps more than any other product in the world, sell by word of mouth. That word of mouth isn't going to happen without that particular voice that turns mere information into communication. Do everything in your power to let your readers know that you are thinking about their needs as you write, and speak to them in a voice that invites them in and gives them confidence.

Don't be afraid to express your empathy for your reader's feelings as he or she is reading challenging passages of your book. We have to make certain assumptions when we do this, of course, the main one being that the reader is engaged in whatever the subject is that we have been discussing, or are getting ready to discuss, at that moment. Here's one example of this, borrowed from my friend Katherine Q. Revoir's book *Spiritual Doodles and Mental Leapfrogs*. In this passage, she is introducing us to an exercise for getting in touch with our inner critics and moving into a positive frame of mind regardless of what these critics are saying:

> When you get a new idea or start to challenge yourself, do you ever hear unwelcomed yet familiar VOICES reminding you of your so-called limitations, past failures, and/or general lack of knowledge or ability? It's hard to be present with yourself when these voices are chattering on and on. . . .[4]

Note that the author does not try to talk us out of what we are feeling in response to these voices. Instead, she acknowledges the voices and also lets us know that they make it "hard to be present" with ourselves. The voice of the author, in this case, is one of understanding, of caring about your life and what you may be experiencing. We perhaps say to ourselves, "Ah, what a relief! This is someone who understands what I go through every time I try to start something new."

Another excellent way of creating a voice of understanding is to tell a story about yourself that shows how you relate to other people in your life. Here's an example from Christina Baldwin's book *Calling the Circle*:

> I believe that my most significant achievement in the first half of my life has been to restore my personal sanity: I am a functioning human being. I know how to think. I know how to feel. I know how to solve problems. I know how to communicate. I am willing to hold myself accountable. I can be in relationship. I practice prayer. This is what I have to offer the world.[5]

With these seventy-two words, we're taken into the author's life for a moment as she reflects on what she values about her achievements at that point in her life. As you can see, it doesn't take a lot, in this case just these few lines, to let the reader know that here is a person who counts the value of her life not in terms of what she owns or what she's accomplished in the external world but in terms of who she has become and what she, standing alone as one person among many, has to offer.

Finally, I offer the voice of Dawn Callan, from her book *Awakening the Warrior Within*. Here she is talking about the way we tend to isolate ourselves from others, and what we can do to let others into our lives a little more. In this instance, the author uses self-disclosure, allowing us to know that she has struggled with this issue in her own life, and so knows of what she speaks:

> Because of the way I grew up, I developed the habit of never asking for help. My credo was to do it all myself, to refuse help even when others offered it. Every time I violated this internal agenda, disaster struck. More often

> than not, it wasn't just a shoe that dropped, the hammer dropped.[6]

Self-disclosure, when it is focused on an issue you are teaching in your book, accomplishes a lot in terms of the "voice" we're exploring here: (a) you tell the reader that you are no stranger to the issue you're discussing; (b) you become a model for the reader, giving hope that they, too, can work this issue through, just as you did.

Let Your Own Soul Be the Example

In his book *One Bowl,* which is about establishing inner harmony in our diets, Don Gerrard suggests that we use journaling to get in touch with past experiences that we have had around food and eating. To show how this is done, he takes the time to share an excerpt from his own journals. I give a portion of that example here as a model of how detailed such self-disclosure can be:

> At our family gatherings, my grandmother always announced the beginning of the meal. . . . As I look back on it, the grand entrance of the food seemed almost like the trumpets announcing the king's entrance in a Shakespearean play, or the tune "Hail to the Chief" announcing the arrival of the president of the United States. It was a triumphant moment—at this point it

> [was] clear that the food [was] the possession of my grandmother and anyone else who had a hand in preparing it. This gift from my grandmother to everyone was acknowledged through proper compliments from the guests: "Mm-m-m. It smells so good! Look at that. It's beautiful!" [7]

These reflections from the author's own journal reveal something about the author. We feel closer to him. We experience a little of his life voyeuristically. His example from life is appreciated, of course, for it provides us with clues for what to look for in our own history. But beyond that, the author's self-disclosure convinces us that he has had these experiences and done this work himself—he knows of what he speaks. We are able to identify with him rather than seeing him as a high-and-mighty expert. He is accessible and human. After all, most of us will be more likely to go where others have gone before us, while we may resist going into places none have gone before. Self-disclosure is like a light in the darkness for your readers, giving them courage to say, "This is possible. Others have traveled this path before me. I can do this."

Laugh and the World Laughs, Too

The Dalai Lama nearly always has a big smile on his face, and his warm chuckle is ever-present. People who have spent much time around him say that even in the midst of reflecting on the most serious world crises there is hardly a moment when he does not project a sense of childlike delight and humor. There are great lessons to be learned from the Dalai Lama's humor, for smiles and laughter are always reminders of how absurd life can be. When I refer to the power of humor, I am not talking about empty jokes meant to distract. Behind humor like the Dalai Lama's are precious insights into our ability to shift our perspectives for a moment and to transform what we are feeling. As my friend Hugh Prather says, "Be a little funny, a little relaxed, a little bit off guard. Sink back into your inherent pleasantness and gaze kindly at the world. The world is indeed a very funny place." [8]

Can you freely exercise humor in a serious spiritual book? Sure, why not? I don't mean that you should break away from the basic instructions to tell a knock-knock joke that has nothing to do with the subject at hand. Rather, look for ways to use humor to lighten the moment, to relax readers and remind them that life can be met with laughter. But do so in a way that keeps the theme of the moment on target. Here are some reasons to use humor:

- Humor can free us to express difficult emotions, to stand outside our fears, our shame, or dark emotions that could otherwise block spiritual growth.

- By softening the impact of difficult emotions, humor can

allow us to open up to others and deepen our sense of contact with other people.

- Humor can change the level of anxiety and tension we're feeling, allowing us to approach an exercise that asks us to stretch beyond our comfort zone.

In the Sufi tradition, humor and irony are at the core of many teaching stories, for they can alter our perspective, allowing us to view the world, or a specific situation, in a new light. One of my favorite Sufi stories, which I've heard many times, is also one of the shortest Hodja tales:

> One morning, Nasreddin Hodja awoke and announced to his wife: "Last night in my sleep a voice whispered to me, 'There is no such thing as voices whispering to you in your dreams.'"

Often these stories point out life's contradictions, or they force us to step back into the role of a witness-observer where we can let go of ego attachments that may have been preventing us from looking at our own lives more honestly. Humor helps us detach from life's unsettling moments and see the larger truths beyond the moment.

Can you imagine a better medium for deepening an insight, fostering and supporting change, or taking in material that is brand-new to you?

It's all too easy to lose sight of the infinite possibilities of the human spirit. Easier still to take a too linear route in our writing, sticking pretty much to stodgy writing that has only limited appeal. But the authors of the best books, the ones that are most successful in the marketplace, know enough to appeal to the individual psyche in a variety of interesting and deserving ways. We'd all do well in our writing to remind ourselves that our readers are far more complex than even they themselves might imagine. The human consciousness is neither an object nor a process; at its best, it is an opening through which the absolute, that is, a Higher Power, is constantly manifesting.

Ultimately, our responsibility as spiritual book writers is to remind our readers of their own courage and their capacities for knowing, and then get out of the way for them to do the rest.

Chapter Seven

Exercises That Grab Your Readers' Attention

Not knowing, and learning to be comfortable with not knowing, is a great discovery.

—Sue Bender, *Plain and Simple*

If you are writing a book on spiritual development, chances are good that most publishers will want you to include experiential exercises to help your readers integrate the concepts you're presenting into their everyday lives. You might want to offer guided imagery exercises, or special meditations, or breathing exercises, a prayer, an affirmation, or the directions for doing a physical posture, as in yoga. How you present these can make the difference between your readers enthusiastically diving in or skipping over them because they look too bland, too difficult, or simply uninteresting. Even if you are writing down an exercise for your own use, such as one you've learned during a retreat, or from a lecture, how you write it can determine whether you want to go back and actually do the exercise or abandon it entirely.

Chances are that you are familiar with the bone-numbing

style of most instructions that come with computers or with your kid's department store bike: *Hit Control key and F1 for help.* Or, *Place washer "d" on bolt "a." Align with hole "FW-3" in fender and screw into threaded hole on underside of steering fork (fig. D-3, page 7).* And we are all aware of the instructions that come with certain products made overseas, written, it would seem, by first-year English students: *Prohibit to use electric device in bathtub or shower for the event of serious injury or death.* If you weren't suffering from utter confusion before reading that stuff, it's a sure thing you would be afterward.

The truth is there are books on spiritual development that aren't written a whole lot better. About a year ago I received a manuscript by a yoga teacher that, oddly enough, was written as if the body, its parts, and all its functions were somehow detached from any form of consciousness. For all that she might have wanted to convey about energizing and integrating body and mind, the instructions she offered left one with the impression that she was describing the lifeless forms found in a mortician's cooler. The following three sentences are examples from that manuscript, offered as models of what *not* to do:

> Assume Lotus position and fill the lungs fully, three times each from first the left nostril, then the right nostril, exhaling the breath fully each time. The belly should swell with each of the inhalations, with the second chakra, being energized, allowing the spine and the head to extend and expand. The subject should begin to feel

> the body energy moving from the base of the spine to the top of the head.

Follow models like this, and in spite of your sincerest efforts your book will languish in your own files for many years, unread and unappreciated except by friends and students who are trying to be polite! However, this kind of writing is far simpler to transform than you might imagine. Notice in the example how the article "the" is working—*the* body, *the* lungs, *the* breath, *the* second chakra. Those articles objectify and distance us from our bodies. If we're to bring them to life—energize them—we need to reconnect them, with language that acknowledges they are integral to our being. Change the articles to personal pronouns and suddenly these disconnected body parts and functions come alive. Here's how the rewritten passage might read:

> As you assume a Lotus position, relax and inhale until you feel your lungs are full and expanded. Do this three times each, from first your left nostril, then your right, exhaling fully each time. Your belly should swell with each of your inhalations. As you do this, you are energizing your second chakra and allowing your spine to extend and expand. You'll soon begin to feel your body energy moving much more freely, from the base of your spine to the top of your head. You may begin to feel sensations of warmth, tingling, increased vibrancy, or other subtle changes that are unique to you. . . .

Writing good self-help instructions is an art. When well written, you'll find them to be engaging, entertaining, intellectually inspiring, educational, and even sensual. Moreover, you don't necessarily stop reading, put the book down and actually *do* the exercises the author describes. Were you to do that, it might interrupt the sense of intimacy we explored in the earlier chapters. Therefore, as the author, you want to write the instructions or exercises so that readers feel free to set their own pace for doing the exercises. In fact, this is one of the tenets of writing good how-to—that readers should never feel they have to put the book down immediately and do the exercises. The only exception might be a book that requires a lot of journaling work. Even then, you shouldn't require your readers to go back and forth between reading and writing in their journals.

If you want to have lots of experiential exercises, pace them so that they come at the ends of chapters. Tell readers at the start of the book that you recommend reading a single chapter at a sitting and doing the exercises only after they complete the reading. In this way the reader can stay focused on one activity or the other—either reading or doing exercises. A book that's paced in this way also gives readers the sense that they are participating in a *program*, that is, in a plan of action, stretching over time, that will help them make important changes in their lives. Indeed, that's the point: They are in fact participating in such a program! Any knowledge that changes how we experience our lives can be classified that way.

Be There for Your Readers

Reading is a very private affair, in fact, much more private and solitary than most activities. If you're the author, you want me, your reader, to become immersed in your book. You want me to surrender myself to your world, and once involved in this way I will be so engrossed I won't want to step back into my own world. This is as true for a good spiritual and personal growth book as it is for a thriller novel. I believe it is important to honor this fact, even when you're in the midst of writing your exercises or other instructive materials. Especially then, keep in mind that your readers will one day take up the book you are writing, fluff up the pillows on the couch or bed, lean back and surrender to reading what you have to say. When that day comes, you want to *be there for them*. I'm not joking about this. You want to make sure that you've written your book so that your readers have the illusion that you are right there with them, supporting them, leading the way, assuring them that if they do get stuck you will not let them stay stuck for long.

If you are writing with the sense of taking responsibility for your readers, as we have discussed in chapter one, you will have no trouble with this. Readers will feel your concern for them, and feel your caring presence. At the same time, the how-to material you write can either break that spell or strengthen it. The following can help you do the latter.

Author-ity Born of Grit and Grease

I found one of my early inspirations for writing how-to material in, of all things, an auto repair manual from the early '70s, titled *How to Keep Your Volkswagen Alive*, written by John Muir. This wasn't the John Muir who wrote all those books about trees, birds, blue skies, and life on the wilderness trail. The one I'm talking about wasn't without appreciation for such things, a fact that comes out in his book, but it's clear that he loved those early Volkswagen Beetles at least as much as he loved nature.

You may be asking, what can a book on auto repair possibly have to teach us about writing a spiritual book? I chose this book as an example for two reasons: first, it graphically reveals how to write truly engaging and personal how-to material, and second, its author, though speaking about auto mechanics, maintains a relationship with his readers that reflects his awareness of the principles of the perennial philosophy.

What John Muir of Volkswagen repair fame taught me, first and foremost, was that whether you are writing a general narrative, an anecdote, or how-to material, you can maintain your intimate connection with the reader and keep the writing interesting. All you have to do is stay alert to the fact that what your book is about is creating a relationship with your readers in which they can take in what you have to say, mingle it with their own knowledge, and end up with the belief that this process was beneficial.

Early on in his book, Muir provides us with a very clear introductory statement about the quality of the relationship we can expect with him. He says, "I am a man, engineer, mechanic, lover-feeler who has worked and felt with cars of all descriptions for many years. This book contains the product of those years: clear and accurate Procedures to heal and keep well your Volkswagen. I don't expect you to become a mechanic—I have done that! My understanding and knowledge will be yours as you work. You supply the labor, the book will supply the direction, so we work as a team, you and I."[1]

You can't get much clearer than that! Out of this clear statement of our relationship with the author, we readers begin to feel a sense of security that *together* we can do whatever we are called upon to do in this mutual endeavor of ours. That's certainly the relationship we want to establish in writing a spiritual book, so maybe this guy has something to teach us after all.

John Muir's writing demonstrates the importance of continually assuring your readers, through details in your writing, that you not only have been where they are right now but that you care enough about their welfare to put yourself back in their place. On page eighty-three of my grease-smudged copy of Muir's book—which, by the way, helped me nurse my well-worn 1971 Beetle through the first five or six very lean years of my writing career—he offers instructions for adjusting the valves. Now, this is a task that you wouldn't even attempt on the newer Beetles, unless you'd already spent two years in the VW mechanics' training course back in Wolfsburg, Germany. But on the early Beetles you could do it with relative ease and a lot of patience if: (a) you didn't have a grease phobia, (b) you had enough mechanical aptitude to rewire the electrical cord on a pop-up toaster, and (c) you owned or could borrow a copy of John Muir's book and a basic set of tools.

John starts by telling readers what to do to work in relative comfort. He advises you to spread a ground cloth under the rear of the car to protect your backsides from the dirt while you slip under the engine. (For those of you who know nothing about those early Beetles, the engine was in the rear.) He instructs you to put on your stocking cap; this is to protect your hair from oil dripping off the engine. He tells you which tools to take along with you, so that you won't have to keep crawling out from under the car searching through your tool box for the right wrenches. You know exactly what to take with you: 13- and 14-millimeter box-end wrenches, a flat blade screwdriver, a feeler gauge, and a flashlight. He even tells you to be looking toward the right side of the car, which is where you'll be starting your work. What's important to note is that Muir is reconstructing the scene in his own mind so that he can tell you exactly what to expect, what you'll be seeing, where you'll probably find some grease and crud, and what to do about it. These aren't just instructions for how to twist bolts. More importantly, they are instructions aimed at helping you perform each task with ease, precision, comfort, and a minimum of anxiety. Reading him, we feel assured that he wants us to succeed. That kind of care, both to the details of the task and the comfort and security of the reader, is critical, whether you are writing a book on auto mechanics or one on spiritual development.

Follow us just a while longer here: Muir now provides instructions from the point of view of the person lying under the car looking up at the underside of the greasy engine. Not a pretty sight, no, but if you are actually going to do what the instructions say, then what the metal looks like under there, which bolts go to which engine parts, and what kind of wrench to use are all realities you're going to need to face. Muir knows this, of course. With every sentence he writes he convinces us that he knows of what he speaks; he's been there, done that, and now is marching us through the process. He leaves little room for big surprises. By the end, you're convinced you can do it because he has made the whole experience so real for you—thanks to the sense of authority we read in his words—even before you've lifted a wrench.

What becomes clear right away is that instructions like this, told from the vantage point of a person actually following them, could never have been written by a person who'd never done exactly what he is telling the reader to do. In a spiritual book, as elsewhere, never try to tell your readers about something you've never experienced for yourself, unless you are willing to tell them that very truth. Muir builds his readers' confidence by virtue of sharing his own experiences. You don't have to brag, and shouldn't. Just give enough details about the experience you're trying to convey that readers will know that you couldn't have known such things unless you'd been there yourself.

When John tells you that you'll need a 14-millimeter wrench to turn a certain bolt, and you try it, and it works, that tells you he's been there himself. You, the reader, are thus encouraged that you are in good hands, that you can do what John is telling you. (He even convinces you it's fun—grease, skinned knuckles, and all!)

What I appreciate most about Muir's style is that his writing reflects a genuine concern for the reader, or why would he go to all the trouble of describing the gritty details, even down to laying out the ground cloth and donning the stocking cap! As you read the instructions he gives, you cannot help but be affected by the author's level of caring, and you will be encouraged to read on, whether you are actually going to adjust your Volksie's tappets or not.

If you actually do repair your car following Muir's instructions, a certain bond is soon established between you and him, and you may read on just to experience more of that. As if aware of this bond, he tells good stories—like the one about "a sympathetic super-mechanic named Muldoon" or the one about how he (Muir) goes shopping for a new (used) Volkswagen bus after his breaks down. In both cases, these anecdotes give us insights into the kind of man the author is—which is how authors establish trust with our readers—and provide information about subjects as far-ranging as how to handle a roadside breakdown and how to buy a used car.

Can this same level of intimacy and even storytelling be used in writing spiritual and personal development books? The answer, as you have probably already guessed, is that it can, which is exactly why I am spending so much time going over the writing techniques I learned from John Muir. I applied Muir's lessons when writing my book *The Lens of Perception*. In it, I provide an exercise for observing how each of us participates in creating our experience of the world. I tell the reader to sit in the center of a room in her home, choosing a room that she has taken an active part in creating. Surrounded by furniture, pictures, rugs, perhaps knickknacks she has chosen, she is instructed as follows:

> Say to yourself, "I have created all this. I have brought these things into my life, and I have created the pleasure I experience in them."
>
> At first this statement may seem unbelievable or absurd. After all, you have not shaped the wood and assembled that chair across the room. You have not shorn the wool and woven the fabric for the upholstery on the couch where you are lounging. How then could you have created all this?
>
> The point is that you have probably not created the objects you see around you. However, the experience of those objects is your creation. And chances are, the objects that you enjoy in this room would not have been present in this place had it not been for choices you made to bring them there. It doesn't matter if the objects you are enjoying were given to you by friends, or if you

> purchased them yourself, or even if, by chance, you did make them yourself. This space where you are sitting would not have been possible without you. You are the key organizer whether you did that organization consciously or not.[2]

Notice how the instructions anticipate what the reader might be thinking and feeling.

The fact that the author's speculations about the reader are perfectly accurate or not is usually less important than the impression you give your reader that you are thinking about her or him, that you truly have her or his best interests at heart. Remember the example from John Muir's Volkswagen book, where the author anticipates what the reader will be experiencing after sliding under the rear of the car. The same principles apply here: You want to communicate to your reader that you are thinking about what he or she will be experiencing while doing the exercise, whether that exercise is changing the oil on your car or learning to meditate. You're establishing a working relationship between yourself and your reader. After all, much of spiritual teaching and insight has to do with exactly that—the quality of relationship we experience between ourselves and ourselves, ourselves and others, ourselves and our planet, and ourselves and a power greater than ourselves.

In the example from my book *The Lens of Perception*, I try to imagine the reader at home in that special room in her house, sitting in the center of the floor and looking around, noting the blue Afghan thrown over the back of the couch, perhaps given to the reader by a special friend, or the earthen surface of the vase bought four years before at a garage sale, or the warm, beige curtains that filter the morning light through the windows. Is this really what you, my reader, are seeing and experiencing as you read this? Probably not, but because I extend myself to you, attempting to put myself in your shoes, as it were, you do feel my effort to reach out to you.

Notice also that the exercise doesn't demand that you stop what you're doing, put down the book, and do what it says. Rather, you are able to read through it and take it in without leaving the comfort of your chair, couch, or bed. Will you do the exercise in the future? Probably not. But you may never again be able to pass through your special room, or maybe any room, without thinking about what you've read and learned here, and therein lies the message.

Here's another example, from Eckhart Tolle's *The Power of Now: A Guide to Spiritual Enlightenment.* Tolle tells his readers how important it is to be "in a state of permanent connectedness with your inner body." If you do keep your attention focused in this way, he promises, you will be "anchored in the Now." In the following passage, he anticipates what the reader might be experiencing along the way:

> Please examine where your attention is at this moment. You are listening to me, or you are reading these words in a book. That is the focus of your attention. You are also

> peripherally aware of your surroundings, other people, and so on.[3]

Note his observations—that your attention is focused on the author while simultaneously being aware of your surroundings. While you can both read and experience what Tolle is describing—as you maintain an ongoing awareness of your surroundings—you do not have to put the book down to do what the author is asking you to do, that is, to *examine where your attention is at this moment*.

Making this connection with your readers, and establishing this quality of relationship with them, requires only that you imagine what they might be experiencing as they read your words. You don't have to be accurate with the specifics, but you do have to hold your readers' lives in your consciousness. After all, what you say will hopefully be making an impact on their lives, and that's a big thing. Your life and theirs touch through your words. As authors of spiritual material, I think it's important that we give that a great deal of thought.

Trust Your Readers

It's your trust of your readers' ability to work on their own that allows you to write how-to material that is respectful of your readers' processes. If you trust your reader fully, you don't allow yourself to slip into a schoolmarm-ish attitude that implies that your readers must do everything you tell them to do. We've all read that kind of book, where you must do each exercise exactly as described and in consecutive order or else nothing is going to work out right. That might be okay for assembling a bicycle or setting up a computer program or baking a cake, but humans are a bit more complicated than that, particularly when it comes to our own personal change and growth.

The human consciousness has its own magic. Build your book around that magic, not around compliance to a particular way of doing something. For example, you can trust and depend on the reader's imagination to take him where he needs to go. Just as we might imagine ourselves slipping under a Volkswagen engine, following John Muir's descriptions, most readers' imaginations will take them to those places you might describe in a spiritual book. Want them to explore the inner world of their own consciousness? Imagine them doing that, as Tolle has done, and they'll tend to go there with you—not exactly as you might imagine but, more importantly, within their own terms and abilities.

Trust the human consciousness—yours and your readers'—to go deep into the inner world of imaginary experiences. Your readers don't have to go to a thirty-story rooftop. All you need to do is have them picture it in their mind's eye: They enter an elevator. The door closes. They feel the floor bounce under their feet, then the increased tug of gravity in their legs as lights over the door jump from one to four to twelve to twenty, and then thirty, where the floor comes to an abrupt stop, giving them butterflies in their stomachs. And then the doors open to the sky.

Now take this little imaginary journey: You are the reader. You cross the hot roof, approach the outer edge of the roof, and then lean over, clinging carefully to the knee-height wall of dirty brick. Thirty stories down the street is filled with tiny cars. They look like toys scooting about. People on the sidewalk are no bigger than ants. Suddenly, a gust of wind pummels your body and your hand slips from the brick wall. Your heart races. Your palms sweat. You push back from the edge, moving to safety.

Want proof that these writing techniques can really engage your readers and keep them eagerly reading? Just look back and note how everything you've read from the beginning of this chapter was, in fact, how-to material. And the elevator ride that I just described? It was intended to have you experience, first-hand, the power of the imagination to trigger some of the same sensations as a real-life experience might do.

The style of writing I'm describing here is just that, a *style*, a way of writing that first and foremost is *experiential*. When well done, it can be as engaging as the best crafted novels that take you into different worlds, even ones you would never go into in real life. As you consider this, remember the second principle of the perennial philosophy, which suggests that it is not just intellectual knowledge of the Divine Ground that we are seeking but the direct knowing of that ground, available to us through imagination and intuition. When we are engaged at these deeper levels, we no longer feel separate from Divine Ground but wholly a part of it.

Chapter Eight

Where Your Journal Can Take You

> *Journal writing is a voyage to the interior.*
>
> —Christina Baldwin, *One to One*

Many writers employ journaling as part of their daily practice, so it seems appropriate to discuss it here, particularly in reference to the ways you might integrate it with writing a book. Private writing, that is, writing intended only for our own eyes, is a natural part of both creative and spiritual evolution. To write in solitude, without the pressures of publishing or the self-consciousness of sharing your work with another person, frees us to express our innermost feelings, explore ideas, and reflect on the daily events of our own life experiences. It offers a venue for working out practical ways to apply spiritual teachings, as well as figuring out how we might change a present behavior to be more in alignment with our spiritual beliefs.

If you're a person who has kept journals for several years, you may have also found it useful to read and reflect on entries you've made in the distant past. Comparing them with today's reflections you can often offer a perspective on the changes you've made over a period of years. Change, after all, is usually quite gradual, even so gradual that we don't notice it's occurred until we are able to compare differences over a long span of time. Your journals can provide you with a deeper appreciation of the time it can take to effect personal and spiritual growth, and your readers will appreciate that. Your own entries can also provide you with anecdotes and insights from your own experience that you can bring to your book, giving authenticity to anything you might write.

Journaling I: Writing in the Present

If you are not presently journaling, now is a good time to start. As we go along, we'll be exploring how this work can be instrumental for writing your book.

Step One: Choose a Journal You Like

There's a wide variety of bound journals available at bookstores and stationery stores, from the simplest and most practical, paper-bound journals to hardcover, leather-bound books with fancy paper. Choose one that you'll enjoy holding and recording your entries in. My only caution is that you find one in which the pages lie flat, making it easy to write in. A friend once gave me a wonderful gift of a journal with a tooled leather cover and beautiful handmade paper inside. It was a work of art. However, the paper had a rough texture that was not easy to write on, and the binding was so tight the pages would not lie flat. Sadly, I made only a few entries in it, then set it aside in favor of a much more *sensible* one, though not half as elegant. Lesson #1: Be sure to get a journal that is easy to write in.

Step Two: Make Daily Entries

I spend at least fifteen minutes every day writing in my journal, though there are times when I also spend several hours either writing or reading and reflecting. My basic journaling exercise is something I call "Writing in the Present." Here's how that works.

Sit down and write for five minutes, doing nothing more than recording whatever is happening in the present. This can be whatever you observe in the external environment around you or whatever is happening within. For example, on a dull day you might start by writing the following:

> **August 7, 2002**
>
> I can't think of a thing to write about today. I am feeling as dull and uninspired as I've felt in months. As I write these words, I become critical of my own handwriting. Today it is sloppier than usual. I wonder if I'll be able to read what I've written a month from now. . . .

On a more inspired day, you might write something like this:

May 17, 2003

I am looking out the window of the small room I've rented for two weeks alone on the Mendocino coast. Directly outside is a beautiful wild flower garden with lavender and roses and a hedgerow of giant daisies. A large brown cat stalks a humming bird that darts from flower to flower. . . .

Sometimes your entries will be very internal:

October 30, 1998

It has been nearly a year now since Mother's death and as I look back, remembering those last days we spent together, it seems to me that she was more peaceful in her own life, as well as in the knowledge of her own passing, than I'd ever seen her. I think her peacefulness allowed me to be more present with her and to enjoy her company, even knowing her life was coming to a close. In many ways, I think, that time we spent together was perhaps the highest quality time we'd had together since I was a small child. . . .

I like to look upon this basic exercise as a "writer's meditation," since in doing it we become more focused on the present—which is, after all, the place where our best writing comes from. And it is also that inner space where we find ourselves suddenly immersed in the creative act of writing. A friend who is an athlete calls it "the writing zone." In sports, he explained, the zone is that space where you're totally in tune with every move you make. You're nearly invincible, and you perform as if you can do no wrong. In journaling, being in the writing zone means that the material effortlessly flows from within, almost magically. Try this writing in the present for a week and you'll see what I mean.

Writing in the present will also reveal to you the various levels of *distance* we may be from the immediate physical presence. For example, in my second example, the writer is observing the immediate physical environment and by so doing is probably, at least for this time, living very much in the *now*. In the first example, the writer is observing the inner environment—i.e., she is feeling dull, not inspired, and is self-critical (she notes that her handwriting is so sloppy she fears she won't be able to read it later on). While her focus is on the present, that is, what is going on in her mind, she is not attuned to the *now* of the physical present. In the third entry, the writer is reflecting on an event that happened nearly a year in the past. Certainly his attention is not focused on the physical *now*, but it is nevertheless focused on, and present in, an event that happened in the past.

As a daily *meditation,* writing in the present is a great warm-up exercise. But it will also tell you where your attention is presently focused. Notice as you are writing your book that when you are focused in the physical present—as in the description of the flower garden, the cat, and the hummingbird—you are describing what you perceive through your five senses: sight, sound, touch, taste, and smell. When reflecting on your feelings, you are describing what you perceive internally, and your language tends to become more abstract. When ruminating on something that occurred in the past, you may use a combination of these. And when you are puzzling something out, you are describing your intellectual process.

In most cases, you will best engage your readers through a balance between these three sources of information: the physical (sensory), the emotional (internal), and the intellectual (cerebral). If you want a reader to feel present with you physically, use physical description, such as the color of the flowers, the sight of the cat stalking the bird, etc. If you want your readers to identify with you emotionally, find words that describe emotional states—"love," "fear," "joy," "anxiety," etc. If you want them to identify with you intellectually, use words that describe intellectual concepts—"conflict," "harmony," etc.

Your writing-in-the-present exercise is an excellent teacher, telling you where you are focusing your attention and telling you how to balance your writing among the emotional, intellectual, and the physical orientations. It has been my experience that writing in the present on a regular basis, and diligently observing the principles I describe here, can help you better understand not only where your attention is focused at any given time but also how to draw in and more fully engage your readers. Study not only the *subjects* of your journal writing but *how* you have written about them, that is, which of these three areas of focus you generally give your attention.

Journaling II: Recording Observations

As you focus your attention on writing your book and start recording your writing experiences in your journal, you may begin to feel that you are attracting help from many unexpected sources. The focused attention seems almost to be like a psychic magnet, if you will, that draws to you information, experiences, other writings, conversations, events, organizations, and individuals that contribute much to your book, even without your asking.

Here's a good example: About a month into writing this book, I ran across the quote by Christina Baldwin, which I've used as an epigraph at the beginning of this chapter. At the time, I didn't know how I would use it, but something told me to save it. (It was only later that I decided to include this chapter on journaling.) About a month later, I was speaking with a client who was just finishing a book she was writing. She told me that she had started journaling using the writing-in-the-present exercise she'd learned in a seminar she'd attended. The daily writing in her journal had then led to the idea for the book she was writing. When I told her that I was writing a book on writing spiritual books, she said I just had to include this chapter on journaling.

"That simple little exercise you call writing in the present taught me to be more observant about where I'm focusing my attention," she said. In that way, she discovered that what she had once thought were writer's blocks were actually the result of being distracted by something that was on her mind. By giving five or ten minutes of attention to the distraction, she cleared her mind of the distraction and freed herself to give her full attention to writing.

Between that serendipitous conversation and the Christina Baldwin quote, I was convinced that I should include this journaling chapter. And, since I'd had the foresight to jot Christina's quote down in my journal, I saved myself the trouble of having to look it up again.

Were we to attempt to remember all the ideas that come up, and that we think we might one day use in a book, we would surely drive ourselves mad. For that reason, if no other, I recommend keeping your journal close at hand and using it as a place to record material that you might use at a later date. If you are jotting down quotes from other people, be sure to reference their sources. It will save you a great deal of work later on. Remember that you will need to provide sources in your book for all quoted material.

Journaling III: Notes to Myself

Some years ago, Hugh Prather wrote a book titled *Notes to Myself.*[1] I liked that he used his journals to express insights, articulate difficult thoughts, and give himself reminders and pep talks. For example, he writes, "To achieve great things we must not only work hard but also dream, not only plan but also believe." At another time he notes, "I talk because I feel, and I talk to you because I want you to know how I feel."

Talking to yourself, particularly in the process of writing a book, can help you through periods of doubt, on those days when the challenge of words seems beyond your reach. Write down what you are feeling, speaking as honestly about your feelings as you can. Be with those feelings, remembering that the only way around them is through them. Then ask Spirit for guidance and perhaps a little courage. There are days of doubt for every writer. Learning to work your way through them is one of the tools of the trade, and your journal can become the companion who helps you through difficult times.

Some years ago I was reviewing journals I'd written many years ago. There were entries where I described some of the same doubts I was currently having. My first response was to criticize myself: "You've still got the same hang-ups you had way back then." But then I saw a different side of it. The fact that I'd been through these doubts many times before and had always found my way out gave me courage. I went even further than that. I patted myself on the back for finding a path through my periods of doubt. Everyone has bad days. Knowing that you've been there before and that you will get to the other side of it soon makes those times a lot easier.

Writing spiritual books requires us to confront ourselves again and again, particularly on those issues we're taking on in our books. Our readers can tell if we really know the territory we're talking about. Our journals are great proving grounds, if you will, where we can go to work out, or work on, those issues that cause us the greatest trouble. What we learn and express there helps to build a foundation for our more mature work. Our private writings will sometimes make it into our books, but just as often they won't, or at least won't appear to. But like everything else in life, our greatest strengths are built upon a foundation that, while invisible, gives our voice a sense of authority and wisdom that otherwise would not be there. The stones and mortar of that foundation can frequently be traced to our journals, to the dark nights of the soul and the moments of bliss that only we need to know about.

Journaling IV: Dreaming

Dreams have played an important part in my spiritual life, for as long as I can remember. Even as a child I delighted in my dreams; they enriched my life and provided me with entertainment. My parents used to say that even my nightmares were a source of wonder for me. I'd describe them over breakfast as if I were retelling a scene from a book or a movie. I never thought of them as revealing anxieties and fears I could not otherwise express, for to me, through my dreams, I entered another world that was as much a part of my life as any other. Many years later I would learn more about this approach to dreams and take it a step further.

In my early thirties, I spent a year or more in Jungian therapy. During that period of time I dreamed I was sitting in a crowded audience watching a theater production taking place on a circular stage. I wore a headset with earphone and microphone, through which I could talk to the actors. Halfway through this play I realized that even though I did not know what was going to happen next on the stage, I was the audience, the playwright, the director, the stage, and the players on the stage. I was both the dreamer and the dream.

My therapist asked what I thought this dream was about. My only answer was that it seemed to be a metaphor for life, that even while we literally create the reality we experience, most of the time what happens is surprising to us. My dream seemed to reflect on the fact that there is an exchange between ourselves and the outside world, represented by the actors, that changes everything, that creates twists and turns that we can't possibly create only on our own. Being able to accept the fact that we create all that occurs in our dreams and in our inner worlds is important. It is also important that we learn to see how we project all this to the outer world, the reality that exists separate from us. Clearly, beyond the stage where my dream took place there was a reality greater than mine that had an impact on me and I on it. At the time, I had no idea how to express this greater reality. Though I didn't recognize it at the time, the dream was a tiny opening, introducing me to the ultimate mystery that embodies all and everything.

Years later, while reading C.G. Jung's work, I found this quote, which seemed to confirm the early explanation for my dream: "This whole creation is essentially subjective, and the dream is the theater where the dreamer is at once scene, actor, prompter, stage manager, author, audience, and critic."[2] Those words rang true for me and gave me a new perspective on how to work with my dreams. Rather than attempting to interpret them, as I'd begun doing in psychotherapy, I would simply record them, checking back from time to time to read them again. Against the backdrop of life experiences over a period of time, the dreams often revealed deeper truths to me—sometimes about my own fears, sometimes about goals and aspirations toward which I was moving.

I don't think I ever would have forgotten that dream, for it marked a turning point in the way I thought about my inner life. But today I treasure the journal, which I still have, that contains that entry. Like an important archaeological artifact, it captures the excitement of a turning point in my personal history, a time when I began seeing how my experience of the outer world is influenced by the inner reality I project to it.

Here's another example of how a journal entry was important to me, and that I offer as an example that can become invaluable in meeting the challenges of everyday life as well as of your writing:

For three years before my father died my dreams prepared me for how I would handle that event. At first I resisted what the dreams said, not wanting to think about my father's death. But as I opened up to the truths they contained, it was impossible for me to deny what they were telling me. I saw that they described ways I could assist him in his death, and how I could help the rest of the family—including myself—through that ordeal. What the dreams told me was that, on the day I heard he was dying, I would turn to my journals and find guidance for how I would handle things when I was called upon.

When the news of Father's death came, I was taken completely off guard. I did not remember the journals at first. But then, as I sat down in my office to decide what I was going to do, an inner voice told me to turn to my journal entries about my father's death. They would tell me exactly what I must do. I followed that guidance, found the journals in question, and the entries were of tremendous help. I believe today that if I had attempted to interpret the dreams, or analyze them by more conventional psychotherapeutic techniques, I could have missed the down-to-earth, practical, and caring support that Spirit provided through those dreams. The direction the dreams gave was both practical and empathetic.

Having those journals in my possession even today is precious to me, both because those entries document that whole process and because they are available to me any time in the future, whether it be to help me meet the challenge of death or to offer a powerful example for a book.

For that reason, I advise you to use your journals to record whatever dreams you can remember, but do this lightly. Do *not* try to interpret them. At least, do not use those dream interpretation books that have become so popular. Respect the inner processes of your own consciousness. Leave room for the mystery that is so much a part of the inner world from which our dreams spring.

Each of us creates our own language of dream symbols unique to us but perhaps containing a larger message than something about our emotional states. By looking at our dreams as stories similar to the mythologies that express the hidden truths of a whole culture, we will find that the fantasy worlds that play out during sleep may express truths about our lives that cannot be reduced to mere reflections of our emotions. Explore your dreams simply by recording them in your journals and then reading them back from time to time as you might read parables, allegories, or legends. Probe the spiritual lessons they might contain even as you look for practical meaning.

As you approach your dreams in this way, you'll find that most offer a spiritual element that is deepened as you simply record them and review them from time to time. When dreams come, or you remember them, record them with as many details as you can possibly remember. Leave yourself open to the stories they tell rather than limiting yourself to dream interpretation methods. Remember that nobody knows the language of your dreams better than you, since each of us creates our own unique symbols and characters.

Journaling V: The Wisdom in Relationships

A Course in Miracles tells us that our relationships are one of our greatest teachers. We learn through the conflicts and joys of relationship all the great spiritual lessons of life: we learn about projection, compassion, and forgiveness, as well as how to give and receive. To those ends, journaling experiences we have in our relationships can be invaluable. By recording as objectively as we can the issues we find ourselves dealing with in our relationships, we are often led to the spiritual lessons we are here to learn.

In their book *Change Your Mind, Change Your Life,* authors Gerald Jampolsky and Diane Cirincione write: "From a spiritual viewpoint, relationships can be seen as laboratories of life where we discover what unconditional love is really all about. The purpose of relationships is seen as an opportunity to learn how to heal the illusion of separation and to experience all hearts and minds as one. In this laboratory of life we discover how to transform fear, guilt, and blame into love."[3]

If you are in a conflict with your life partner, a coworker, a friend, or anyone else in your life, take a look at what that conflict might tell you. The problem might even be with a person you do not consider important at all, such as a telephone solicitor who has interrupted your dinner. For example, in the middle of enjoying dinner with friends one evening, the phone rang and I answered it, expecting a call from a friend who had announced he'd be late. Instead, it turned out to be a telephone solicitor selling long-distance phone service. I was annoyed and said something that was undoubtedly quite rude before slamming down the phone on him.

As I turned to rejoin my friends, the phone rang again. I picked it up, certain it must be our missing friend this time. Instead, I heard the voice of the solicitor who'd called before. "Listen," he said. "I want to tell you something. I take a great deal of pride in what I do. I am sorry that it's an inconvenience to you, I really am. But this is the way I support my family, and I make no apologies to anyone for that."

I was flabbergasted, but I heard every word he said. There was a short pause on the line as he completed what he had to tell me, and then I replied, "I understand. And I apologize. I am truly so sorry."

"Thank you," he said, softly, before hanging up, perhaps moved as much by my apology as I'd been moved by his protest of my rudeness.

There was certainly a lesson in this, for it was a reminder that I hold in my heart even to this day, that all relationships matter, no matter how fleeting or seemingly insignificant they might seem to us. This man's courage to call back caused me to recognize, in a very real way, that every relationship is an opportunity to learn. But who would have ever imagined that a telephone solicitor interrupting my dinner would be my spiritual teacher that day?

Use your journal to record moments such as this. But don't overlook the everyday relationships with those around you: family members, coworkers, and friends. Each of them has the potential to mirror back to us the lessons that we most need to hear. All the lessons of your journal will likely make it into your other writing one day, so treasure what you record there, and think of your journals as the valuable writer's resources that they are.

As you work with your journal, you'll develop your own methods and style of working. While the suggestions above give you a place to start, don't feel bound by them. What's most important is that you develop a way of using your journal that will work for you. In the best of all worlds, the thought of sitting down with your journal at the beginning or end of the day would excite you and would, over time, become a valuable self-reference for your writing as well as your own spiritual growth.

Chapter Nine

Getting Paid to Write Your Book

If you have a salable idea, prepare a proposal, and sell it, you will no longer be just a writer with an idea. You will be an author, as in authority, with a book to your credit.

—Michael Larsen, *How to Write a Book Proposal*

According to most publishing experts, approximately ninety percent of all nonfiction books are sold to publishers, prior to the manuscript being finished. On the basis of a good proposal, a publisher will offer you not only a contract to publish your book but, if you're lucky, an advance against your future royalty earnings to write it. For a first-time author of a spiritual book, those advances are usually not large. But it can mean having at least a few weeks of freedom to put the finishing touches on your book without having to worry about paying for groceries and the rent. If you've got a book that a mainstream publisher can't resist, and if the publisher believes you'll be able to promote and sell your book, the advance can be much more than that . . . MUCH more.

Many authors find that writing a proposal is as much work as writing the whole book. On the plus side, proposal writing forces you to think through every aspect of your book and to write at least two sample chapters to give yourself and an agent or publisher a good taste of what your book will be about. From that perspective, writing a book proposal can be highly creative because you'll be involved with imagining how all the pieces will go together, and along the way you may even think of a better way to write your book.

There are two books on writing book proposals that have become standards in the publishing world. They are Michael Larsen's *How to Write a Book Proposal* and Jeff Herman and Deborah Levine Herman's *Write the Perfect Book Proposal.* Try to get Larsen's third edition (2004), which I recommend since it contains important updated material. These two books not only go into extensive detail about writing proposals (with samples enclosed in both books), but they also have excellent information about the inner workings of the publishing business. All three authors are literary agents, the Hermans on the East Coast, Larsen on the West.

If you plan to write a proposal, I recommend that you get both these books and use them as reference material. If you use even a tenth of what these authors say in these books, you'll be able to write a successful proposal and you'll be perceived by agents and publishers as an author who knows what you're doing.

Because these two books are easily available, I won't go into great detail here, but I will describe the core elements that you will need for putting together a selling proposal. The Hermans' and Michael Larsen's books will give you the finer details.

The Basics

Here are the elements of a standard book proposal:

- **Title Page:** Centered on a single page of its own, your title page should contain the title and subtitle and the author's name.

- **Table of Contents for the Proposal:** This is the table of contents, with proper numbers, telling the reader on which page to find the Introduction to the proposal, including the Overview and About the Author. It should also tell where to find the Chapter Outline of the book and your two sample chapters.

Now let's look more closely at the details of what the proposal itself consists of.

The Introduction

The introduction consists of eight to fifteen pages of material that offer a clear picture of what the book contains and who the author is. Here's how that works:

Overview

This section needs to sell the publisher on the idea for the book and should outline why you think that your book has a potential readership. The first paragraph needs to grab the readers' attention so that they will want to read the rest of the proposal. You might start with an anecdote that captures the essence of the book. For example, the author of a sample proposal in Michael Larsen's book tells the story of a fifteen-year-old daughter whose father contracts cancer. She is not told that he is ill and lives with the mystery of why he slowly withdrew from her life. The story is emotional and enigmatic, a perfect lead-in for a book meant to help friends and family members relate to a critically ill friend or family member.

You might also start the overview with a more objective statement that describes the need for the book. For example, the opening paragraph in a proposal for a book about the retirement years might simply state how many people will be retiring in the next ten years, making a case for the existence of seventy-five million potential buyers.

What then follows in the overview is further discussion of the proposed book and why you believe it will make a successful book.

Markets for the Book

In this section you think of all the potential niches that might constitute buyers of the book. For example, in their book *The Cultural Creatives,*[1] authors Paul H. Ray and Sherry Ruth Anderson present data showing that there are fifty million Americans who hold strong spiritual values but who are not necessarily associated with any religious organizations. Sometimes there are several niches of readers you can anticipate selling your book to. For example, a spiritual book on relationships might be aimed at marriage and family counselors in addition to the general public.

Promotion

Here you will describe to the publisher what you can do to sell the book. What will you do to promote it? Be specific. Do *not* say, "I will do whatever the publisher asks me to do to promote the book." Rather, describe an actual promotional campaign that you might put together. If it looks good to publishers, they will work with you to develop your campaign in most cases.

Name any media contacts that you already have, if any.

If you are presently doing seminars, name that as a promotional venue.

If you are planning to write articles based on the book, or even excerpted from the book, say so.

If you have a way of selling your books, such as through a website or back-of-the-room sales in your seminars, mention that and give an estimate of how many books a year you can sell. (They won't hold you to a specific number, but it's good to give them an estimate.)

Complementary Books

Publishers like to know about any similar books that are already out there in the bookstores. The fact that there are a few out there already helps to establish the fact that there is a market for your subject. Publishers also want some assurance that the market for a book like yours isn't already saturated. In this section you should cite books (title, author, publisher, date of publication) that might be seen as complementing your book. They should be books that have been published in the last three years. Look for books that have been quite prominent. I always look for at least one *New York Times* bestseller to compare my own books with, to show the publisher that there is a big market for the subject. There should be a paragraph or so describing the contents of the competing book and telling how your book is different—that is, how your book offers some *added value* that wasn't in the other book.

About the Author

Beginning writers often make the mistake of being too chatty and informal in this section. For example, I don't know how many times I've read author bios that begin something like this: "I'm mom to a three-year-old daughter named Shelly May, a twelve-year-old, thirty-pound Tabby cat named Rainbow, a standard poodle named Vanilla, and a goldfish named Finny. I manage to write a paragraph or two at a stretch before getting interrupted by one of them. . . . " And so on.

The author bio needs to be focused and to the point, providing only information that relates to the book you are writing or your ability to drum up publicity for your book. I suppose there are books where a bio like Shelly's mom's would strike the right note, but be certain that whatever you write is appropriate for your material.

The Outline

List of Chapters

Here you will simply list your chapters by their numbers and title, for example, "Chapter 1: A Good Beginning." Ideally this list will fit on a single page. Make your chapter titles as descriptive as possible, each one hinting at the contents of its respective chapter.

Working Chapter Outline

The working chapter outline may be the biggest writing challenge in writing a proposal. For each chapter you should have between 200 and 300 words telling what it will contain. Tell only enough to paint a picture of what each chapter will encompass, without going into great details.

Two Sample Chapters

Choose your two most exciting or original chapters to include here. These chapters should be truly representative of your book both in style and the level of information you'll be giving. The length should be at least eight pages but no more than twenty-five per chapter.

Take care in writing your sample chapters. I recommend getting an editor to go over the final draft, to catch all errors and make certain they're corrected. The proposal is largely informational, but don't underestimate the importance of details, such as making certain there are no glaring errors or typos. A polished proposal tells publishers what they can expect from you. Publishers love it when they find a writer who has original ideas, writes well, and pays attention to details. All those qualities mean less work for them, and with the workloads that most in-house editors are carrying these days, that's got to be a high priority.

The proposal serves several functions, not all of which are obvious to the beginning writer. First, it provides evidence to an agent or acquisitions editor at a publishing house that you've spent considerable time thinking about your project and that you know what you are talking about. Second, if the agent likes the proposal, he or she will use it to sell the idea to a publisher.

The agent's main contact with most publishers is the acquisitions editor, whose responsibility it is to find books to publish. The proposal builds on whatever working relationships the agent may have with the acquisitions editor. Third, if the agent manages to sell the idea for your book to the acquisitions editor, that person, in turn, will use your proposal to sell the book idea to an editorial board. Fourth, after you receive a publishing contract, the selling proposal provides guidelines for you to follow in writing the book. While most publishers do not insist that you follow the proposal to the T, they do want to make sure that you'll cover the main items that you promised to cover in your book proposal.

The Query Letter

The usual way of presenting a book proposal is to first send a short letter to prospective agents or publishers describing the book in a way that is intriguing enough to get the publisher or agent interested. Once that's accomplished, send the whole proposal.

The query letter is usually generated from the first few paragraphs of the Overview in your Introduction. Rewrite those paragraphs so that they won't sound quite the same when you send the agent or publisher your complete proposal. It doesn't hurt to include in the query letter a self-addressed stamped postcard (first class) that shows the return address of the agent or publisher you've sent it to. In the message area, have a box the respondent can check off, telling you either that they are not interested in seeing the proposal or that they are.

Further Reading

While I've given you the rudiments, I highly recommend that you get the proposal writing books I've cited and in the "Books for Going Further" section at the end of this book. There are many details that I've had to leave out, given space restrictions in this book.

Chapter Ten

Getting Published and What Comes After

> *Once a book is published, it no longer belongs to me. My creative task is done. The work now belongs to the creative mind of my readers. I had my turn to make of it what I would, now it is their turn.*
>
> —Katherine Paterson, *Gates of Excellence*

There is a point, after the fourth or fifth or maybe tenth rewrite, when you have to accept the fact that it is time to let your book go, to send it off to find its way in the world. This is a major milestone for most authors, comparable to the empty nest syndrome that parents report after their youngest child leaves home. While I admit to having a little fun with it here, the truth is that many authors not only resist putting the finishing touches on their manuscript but also feel a big letdown when they finally ship their book off to the publisher.

On the one hand, you may feel relieved. Your job is done. You no longer have to face that empty page crying for you to fill it with words every morning. No longer do you have to face the computer monitor with its vacant stare. But you also recognize that when the manuscript leaves your possession, it will leave a big hole in your life. After all, it has consumed a great deal of your time and energy for months, maybe years.

You suddenly discover how much of your life has been structured around the production of your manuscript. You spent hours at your desk, writing, researching, reading, maybe even interviewing other people, and then revising, revising, revising. Over dinner, family members have complained that you had always seemed distracted, your mind a million miles away—still immersed in your writing. Even your dreams were filled with the book, with new ideas awakening you at 3 a.m., forcing you to jot down notes on a pad beside your bed or sending you to your computer to write a few pages while everyone else in the world snored quietly in their warm and comfy beds.

For many authors, there's a natural reaction to completing a book. We can think of a million and one things we've forgotten to put in, or that we decide at the last minute to cut. Or we feel compelled to give it, well, maybe just one more close reading to make certain we haven't missed something. Like overprotective parents, we hover over our handiwork, keeping it safely locked away in a drawer where it will be guarded from the harsh realities of the world we know it must eventually face.

For every writer who clings to her manuscript, inventing all kinds of excuses to not let go, there are a dozen more who send their manuscripts out prematurely. For the latter, there's a new kind of danger. The publisher or literary agent they send it to is not able to see beyond the typos or imagine the brilliance of all those yet-to-be-developed concepts. As exciting as the author's ideas might be, the effort to get the incomplete manuscript read is worse than a waste of time. More than that, sending your work out before it's ready is blowing an opportunity, for you may not get a second chance to show the manuscript around.

The only advice I can offer you, if you count yourself in the premature send-off group, is this: Don't let your excitement about your work blind you to the realities of publishing—that literary agents and publishers will be judging your manuscript not on its *potential,* or even on the enthusiasm of the author, but on the quality of writing that is already there. Agents and publishers are part of this process of publishing, and the sooner you recognize your partnership with them, the better. They want the work to be as finished and clean as possible. They don't want to take on a manuscript that is going to add to their present burden, but they know they have a duty to make an author's work publishable, and to shepherd it on to its readers.

Many first-time authors make these errors—either clinging to their manuscripts for one more go-around or sending them out too soon—because they are unfamiliar with the way publishing works. Publishing is, after all, a collaborative affair, with author and publisher working together to turn the manuscript into a book, hopefully one that will be read and sought by thousands of people. But publishing itself is very different from writing, and because the priorities in publishing mostly revolve around running a business, the publishing world can seem quite antagonistic to the creative process of writing, especially to first-time authors. The *cure* for the author is to acquire some solid information about how publishing works and how to handle the conflicts that sometimes arise between the different priorities of publishers and authors. It helps to focus first on the one thing that most authors and publishers hold in common: they both want to reach as many readers as possible. They both want a successful book.

Recognize Differences in Your Shared Interests

While authors and publishers share a common ground, the distance between them can often seem vast. As a first-time author, keep in mind that your publisher has been there a great many times before. In spite of how their priorities can, at times, ruffle your feathers, learn to stay focused on the fact that the best, most successful books are mutual efforts where author and publisher respect their different priorities but join those priorities for their mutual benefit.

Authors and publishers have different reasons for wanting to reach as many readers as possible. For the author, it's usually because he has an important message to share. For the publisher, it's about money. The more readers reached, the more books will be sold and the greater will be the publisher's profits. Most publishers also have a reputation to uphold. They want to be thought of as producing good books, meaning books that get good reviews and also sell well.

It's not that publishers are only in the business of making money, but publishing is a labor intensive and expensive proposition, and if they want to stay in business for long, they've got to sell books. No sales, no publishing company. No publishing company, no place for authors' books to get published. No books, no readers, and so on. I've known many publishers who are as idealistic as any authors I've ever known, but every day that they go into work they must face the reality of how they're going to make publishing a viable business, and sometimes that means leaning on authors a little to broaden their readership. They must keep focused on the fact that success or failure rests on their ability to sell large numbers of books. It's a mass media proposition—meaning that if you are making and selling "low ticket" items, that is, products selling for under $500 each, you've got to sell a lot of them.

The harsh reality is that publishers are producing objects (books) that must compete in the marketplace with other objects that may look and feel very similar. For example, how will they make another book on Buddhism or another book on forgiveness stand out from among dozens of others on the same subject? While you, the author, concentrate on communicating as clearly as possible with your reader, your publisher concentrates on ways to reach thousands of people who are willing to shell out fifteen or more bucks for your book.

For the most part, editors at publishing companies understand their authors' priorities better than authors might imagine. The editor you're working with may know a lot more than you think they do about what it means to be an author. In fact, they might be working on their own books or have a book or two of their own in print. The same goes for literary agents. I would venture to guess that at least a quarter of the editors and agents I've worked with, or at least rubbed elbows with, over the years have also been authors. This includes a few very successful authors, such as Nobel Prize-winner Toni Morrison, who was an editor at Random House for many years. To know that the editor you're working with might well be a fellow author helps to put things in perspective when the publisher's priorities seem to be coming in conflict with your own. Err on the side of optimism. Assume that your editor is an ally, someone who understands the world of writing and publishing from both sides of the desk.

Editors tend to be modest souls. They might not volunteer the fact that they have a book or two of their own in print and that they know what it is to subject their manuscript to an editor's red pen. Treat them as you would a close friend—for they may well become one—by inquiring into their accomplishments. You certainly want an ally at your publisher's, so don't forget the basic spiritual principles of every relationship—for example, that *giving is receiving*. If you have a working understanding of what your publisher needs from you to make a successful book, as well as what your editor needs to do his or her job, you can make the process of getting your book into print a rewarding experience for everyone. Be willing to ask your editor questions such as, "How can I be helpful to you?" One way to do that is to find out exactly what the publisher expects of you.

Great Expectations: Steps on the Way to Publication

I'm writing the following with the understanding that your book is under contract with a publisher. The information hereon is focused on the publishing process per se. While you might have believed your job was done the moment you finished the writing, it's not. Here's what to expect.

Step One: Preparing Your Manuscript for Submission

Most publishers will send you a packet of material titled something like "Guidelines for Submitting Your Manuscript," or "Author Guidelines," or "Submission Package." It will tell you how your publisher wants your manuscript prepared for its final submission package. So that this won't come as a big surprise to you, here's a summary of what I found in the guidelines from five different publishers:

Opening and Salutation

There is usually a greeting, telling something about the publishing company, their philosophy, and the kind of relationship they like to establish with their authors. This section might tell you about the various people who'll be working with you. Most of them you will never meet or even talk with on the phone, but they'll be there. With smaller publishers, more than one of the following functions may be handled by a single person:

Editors and Directors

- **Editor, Editorial Assistant:** This is your main contact person with your publisher. In many cases, all your business with your publisher will be handled by this person.

- **Copyeditors, Production Manager:** With many publishers, you'll never have any direct contact with either of these people, though you will definitely be exchanging work with them. The production manager is the person who keeps everything on track, guiding your manuscript through the production process. Copyeditors are the people who go over your manuscript after all rewrites have been completed, checking for typos and grammar mistakes.

- **Sales and Marketing Director, Publicity Manager:** These are the people who will make the important connections between your book and the sales reps, distributors, and ultimately the booksellers who will in turn sell your book to readers. They manage marketing and promotion, setting up professional conferences when appropriate and organizing special sales through non-bookstore venues and mail-order companies.

Specifications, Style, and Formatting

This refers to any stipulations that were in your contract: word count, any graphics noted there, and any backmatter (index, bibliography, etc.) for the book.

It's generally agreed that authors should follow the *Chicago Manual of Style* for style, punctuation, and usage.

As for formatting, don't do anything fancy. Do *not* try to design the book, adding any special formatting, such as fancy fonts, color, etc. This is important, since the designer and typesetter will be using your electronic files to set up the final design work for the printed pages. They will want the most simple formatting possible so that time will not be wasted converting your manuscript to the more sophisticated formatting software they use.

Publishers hire book designers because they know how to design covers that will both identify the content and attract readers who are interested in the content. Do you have a great idea for the cover? Well, maybe you do and maybe you don't. But leave the way open to listen carefully to what your publisher says about the cover. He or she may know something you don't. Let the designer design. Listen to what they have to say if they offer to let you take a look at what they're developing. Comment on the work, but respect their professional perspectives.

Some years ago, I worked with an author who was somehow convinced that however he submitted his work would be the way it would come out in the book. He added all kinds of fancy fonts and spacing, in spite of his editor's pleas to leave it alone.

Two weeks after submitting his manuscript, the publisher sent it back to him, insisting that he take out every last bit of special formatting he'd put in. He was livid, for he'd spent weeks *designing* his book. Only after seeing the interior designs of other books by the same publisher could he be convinced that it was okay to leave the designing to the designers. If trusting the design to the designers is Hard and Fast Rule #1, here are three more:

Hard and Fast Rule #2: Number pages consecutively.

Hard and Fast Rule #3: Submit everything double-spaced.

Hard and Fast Rule #4: Keep a hard copy as well as an electronic copy of whatever you submit.

Manuscript File

You can assume that your publisher will require you to submit the electronic file of your manuscript in Microsoft Word. PC or Macintosh are both okay, unless you're told otherwise. The reason for this is that this file will be used by the person doing the typesetting, and other software is not quite as compatible with the software typesetters use.

Though I use both Microsoft Word and WordPerfect, I prefer to write in WordPerfect. When I do, I find that when I've finished writing I can easily convert the files to Microsoft Word before submitting them to my publisher. If you are going to do this, just make sure way ahead of time that your conversions are going to work. Some older versions of Apple software, for example, are difficult to convert. Conversion can usually be worked out, but you may have to find someone who has the proper software to do it. Check with your publisher and ask about this.

I once worked with an author who was writing his whole book on a $300 self-contained word processor with a tiny screen. The hard-wired software didn't even have a name. It would have been a problem to convert except that I discovered that his word processor saved all files in Text format on a diskette. I could open the files in Word for Windows, the basic word processor that comes with Windows, save it as a .doc file, and then open and save in Microsoft Word. With a couple hours of correcting the formatting, we were able to get an electronic file that the publisher would accept. Had we not been able to do so, it would have meant hiring someone to retype the whole manuscript. Soon afterward, that author bought a new computer.

Some publishers want you to send the entire manuscript in one long file while others want the book broken down with a separate file, for each chapter. Check on this before submitting. For various reasons, I always work with separate files for each chapter. I then have to string them together into one file for some publishers. Doing so is quite easy with both Microsoft Word and WordPerfect, but if you're not familiar with the process, check with your software manual or your computer tech person.

If you have artwork or photos that go with the text, ask your publisher how to submit them. There are three or four different methods for doing so; make sure you are doing it the way your publisher wants.

Submit a Complete Manuscript

When submitting your manuscript, make sure that you have included all the parts. There's nothing quite as irritating to a publisher as having an author dribble in the bits and pieces of her manuscript over a week or two. Make yourself a checklist, including: table of contents, preface, foreword, dedication page, acknowledgments, and introduction. Do you need all of these? It depends on the publisher and author, of course, but forewords and prefaces are generally optional. Take a look through your library to find out how other authors use these sections and decide whether or not you wish to do the same.

Don't forget endmatter, such as bibliography, appendices, epilogue, and index, if applicable. And if you used long quotes that require permissions, be sure to include releases in your packet.

Step Two: The Editorial Process

You may sincerely believe that you have crossed every "t" and dotted every "i" and that the manuscript couldn't possibly be improved. Were it only true, authors' and publishers' jobs would be a lot easier and they would get into fewer conflicts. But if you've been through the process of publishing at least one manuscript before, you will have come to discover that authors are notoriously blind to their own errors. There are no exceptions

. . . at least I've not discovered any yet. This isn't to disparage authors. What we know about this whole writing and editing business is that they are two very different activities. A writer's focus is on expressing ideas, concepts, and feelings. In the process of bringing all those together, we don't always see typos, misspellings, and grammatical errors. Nor do we always see organizational flaws. Publishers not only understand this about writers, but they plan for it. That's why God invented editors. Here's what to expect:

- **Editorial Review:** When your manuscript comes in, the editor you've been communicating with from the start will read it over for content, general organization, style, and how well you've delivered on the promise of the book. He or she might make suggestions for improving any or all of these. This editing is for the big stuff, to make the manuscript work as a book. You might get a lot of suggestions or a few. You will probably have a few conversations with your editor as you go about making these suggested changes. When both you and the editor are satisfied with the manuscript, it will be passed along to the copyeditor.

- **Copyediting:** It's the copyeditor's job to focus on the picky things, to make sure you've fixed all the things you and your editor discussed. Along the way, he or she will go through the manuscript with a fine-toothed comb, noting any typos or other small errors that you or your editor failed to notice. The manuscript then goes back to you, with all the editorial notes, and it's then your responsibility to enter any changes that have been indicated. You should definitely *not* be doing any new writing at this point, except for what your editors have requested. Now everything goes back to your copyeditor, who'll probably give the manuscript one more read to make certain everything has been done.

Proofreading: Are you getting tired of seeing your manuscript? Yes, probably. In fact, there's a good chance that you know it by heart and at least feel like you could recite it forward and backward. No matter. You're now going to receive "galley proofs," which will be your entire typeset manuscript with all corrections inserted. Sometimes the proofs will be in exactly the form they will appear in the final book. It's now your responsibility to read your book closely one more time before it goes to the printer. Look for errors now. It's too late for any significant changes or additions. If you catch something that really and truly must be fixed, call your publisher immediately and discuss it. Bear in mind, though, this is not the time to get obsessive about tiny changes you wish you'd made when you had a chance. This is the countdown, and you better be ready to go with the lift-off.

A Window into the Publishing World

One of the toughest things about being an author may be the realization that, while writing the manuscript was the center of your attention for many months, your work, as precious as it may be to you, is only one manuscript among many at the publishing house. Editors may have as many as a dozen different projects in production at the same time, with other manuscripts lined up for further review or for consultations with their authors or for negotiations with the authors' literary agents.

With that picture in mind, is it any wonder your phone calls and emails are not always promptly returned? Does this mean you should sit on your hands awaiting a call or email from your editor or someone else at the publisher's? No. If you have questions that are not urgent but that are nevertheless important to you, send reminder notes every week or so, just to keep your place in line. I have to confess that even as a freelance editor, I'm not always good about returning calls or emails. When the pressure is on as the result of a publisher's deadline, for example, that deadline must be given top priority. There are just too many people involved to ignore it. If I return every phone call—even to close friends—or answer the phone on every ring, or reply to every email, there honestly would be no time for writing and editing.

There are days, even for me, when I receive close to 100 emails (not counting spam) and a dozen or more phone calls. It's terribly frustrating to go through those periods, especially when I really do enjoy talking with other writers. What's more, I know that people who are trying to contact me are getting frustrated and angry with me. If there's one piece of advice I can give writers who are having trouble getting their editors on the line, it would be this: Be patient but be tenacious. Put yourself in your editor's shoes and let him know that you do understand his dilemma. After all, you're in this together and neither of you can get along without the cooperation of the other. Keep phone calls brief and to the point when it appears that your editor is rushed or pressured. It may sound preachy to say this, but there are days when the only solution is spiritual—focus on the moment with compassion, forgiveness, and peace of mind.

If there's something truly urgent to communicate to your editor—if, for example, you need to coordinate with them on a publicity date or you have just found a glaring error in the final galleys—ask to speak to someone, anyone, in the editorial office. Tell them your story and chances are good that you can get help that way. What's a good example of something important enough to do this? I offer this anecdote: An author who'd previously given me permission to use a long quote suddenly withdrew her permission without telling me why. I was panicked. I had already turned in the galleys and knew the project had either gone to the printer or was on its way. I knew I'd be able to provide an alternative quote and some new writing that would keep the same page count so I made the emergency call to the publisher, eventually got my editor on the line, and together we worked out a last-minute solution, saving the publisher the cost of having to reformat the entire book.

It's always been my experience that editors are fairly even-tempered souls, with a great deal of patience. They're sticklers on deadlines because they have to be. They know that the late delivery of a finished manuscript can affect the schedules of a great many other people, including printers, who are not at all forgiving about delays. You should also keep in mind that if the book has a set publication date and your publishers can't deliver books to their distributors and booksellers as a result of a delay in production, this can really hurt the sales of the book, even kill the sales entirely in some cases. So take deadlines seriously and be assured that your publisher will be doing the same.

As for the patience of editors, a psychologist friend once pointed out that it's a profession that demands near-perfect mastery of the art of delayed gratification. After all, great spans of time pass between the time an editor acquires a manuscript for her publisher and the day she finally sees the book in print. A person with poor abilities to wait things out could never deal with that.

The downside of this gift is that putting off a phone call for a couple weeks is really no problem to a person who handles delays well. If you, the author, are also good at delayed gratification, this will be no particular problem for you. But if you are a Type A personality who wants everything to happen when you want it to happen, you're going to be tested sorely, not because publishers and their workers don't care about you and your book but because the business of getting a book out is complex and there's plenty of room for things to go wrong. What goes wrong isn't necessarily something with your book, either. It could be that any of the other projects your editor is working with might require more attention than was originally estimated, and that trickles down to everyone.

Step Three: Promotion

Volumes have been written about book promotion, so I won't attempt to do anymore than provide an overview on that subject here. (You'll find further suggestions in the "Resources" section.) Suffice it to say, however, that promotion is Step Three of the business of publishing.

There's a general, if rarely articulated, rule that only books that don't need advertising and promotion get it. While this might seem to fly in the face of common sense, in truth it makes good sense, at least from an economic standpoint. Consider this: The amount of profit a publisher can expect to make on a single book is tiny compared to, let's say, selling TV sets or cars. If money is to be made, it must be made by selling huge numbers. Needless to say, unless a book is seen by the publisher as having a potential market of 50,000 copies or so, there really isn't room for much of an ad budget. And how many books sell 50,000 copies or more? Not many. Most sell 20,000 or less. An experienced publisher gets pretty good at estimating what the readership will be for a book—and that's why ad budgets remain low.

Publishers also know that ads in magazines and newspapers don't sell books. The only time publishers will spend much money for this kind of advertising is when they want to announce a new book by an author whose previous book was a bestseller. Should writers spend money for print ads for their books? My opinion is no. There are more effective ways to promote your book.

You'll probably remember that I've said a couple times before in these pages that books are mostly sold by word of mouth, not by the usual advertising and promotional channels. Successful word-of-mouth promotion happens only when thousands of people find something in your book of sufficient value that they almost can't stop themselves from sharing it with other people.

Because of the nature of word-of-mouth advertising, the success or failure of a book is largely in the hands of the author. This is not to say that publishers don't have a responsibility to do everything in their power to make sure the book sells, but unless the book captures the attention of readers, no matter how good the book, there is no amount of advertising that will rescue it. Publishers send out review copies. They'll put out catalogs that go to buyers at bookstores. They'll maybe even carry your book around to be displayed in their booths at book fairs around the country. Their sales reps, or the reps at their distributors, will be prepped on what your book offers.

My experience, however, especially with spiritual books, is

that the author's contact with his or her potential readers is singularly important. Readers like to make personal contact with authors. As we've discussed elsewhere, spiritual and personal growth books deal with intimate issues. When books of this kind are working well, readers may feel that they know the author well. Being able to be with readers in person, to shake hands with them, or even exchange a hug, can feel as fulfilling to these readers as a visit with a close friend they only rarely see. If we've done our job well as writers, our readers may even feel that we understand things about their lives that nobody else in the world does. Readers may have come to your book for comfort at a difficult time in their lives. They may have found assurance about their own lives, or found direction through a stormy period. At the very least, if they've read your book and benefited from it, they may feel that you have contributed something valuable to their spiritual development.

Knowing all this helps us appreciate what we offer our readers when we go out to make a bookstore appearance, deliver a lecture, or present a workshop. The contact you make with your readers by doing this does help to sell books, but it's also important to your readers, satisfying a need in them to be in the presence of a person who has had an impact on their life. Don't ever underestimate what you offer in this way.

Where and how do you make these contacts with your readers? Your publisher can help with this, giving you names and addresses of bookstores throughout the country that welcome authors for short talks and book signings. Work closely with your publisher on putting your promotion together. This is important.

Many bookstores sponsor short seminars, usually no longer than two days. There are also seminar centers throughout the country that welcome authors who can attract a group of people for longer workshops and seminars. Discuss with your publisher how you might make use of these venues to get the name of your book around. You'll find further suggestions for promotional opportunities in the "Resources" section of this book.

In the spiritual community, small seminars are very popular. If you've written a book, doing seminars is the very best way for you to promote yourself and your book. The book can be advertised along with the seminar, and should be, but it is the seminar that covers the cost of the ad. That's simple economics: the book costs $12 to $30. The seminar costs $75 to $250 or more. It's clear what's going to pay the promotional bill.

In the earliest talks with your publisher, you should broach the subject of who will pay for promoting any workshops you might do. It may turn out that this is your responsibility, but maybe your publisher will hire you a helper as well. Having a book is a great calling card for giving credibility to your workshops and talks. Many authors set up their own workshops, but if you do, make sure you coordinate your efforts with your publisher in case your publisher wants to set you up for some bookstore appearances along the way. Build a mailing list of people who might be interested in your workshops so that you can mail out, or email, brochures that tell people what you are offering. (See "Show Guides" in the "Resources" section for services.)

And let's not forget the Internet. Every author should have a website. There are so many resources on the Internet these days that make this possible. In the Authors Guild author's website program you can build your own site and pay less than $100 a year for hosting (if you are a member). Or you can operate your own domain hosted by a regular Internet server. Again, there are whole books dealing with the creation of websites, and covering all that in the short space we have here isn't reasonable.

Finally, consider adapting your work as short articles that you can send to the hundreds of newsletters, magazines, and Internet 'zines that are published in the United States and Europe these days. A little research on the Internet will turn up a wide selection of publications to choose from, with instructions on how to submit your material. Always be certain you can get a byline and a short blurb that will promote you as the author of your book. It's best to work with your publisher on this, since publishers will usually be a few steps ahead of you, with plans already in motion to sell first serial rights for excerpts from your book.

Is all of this really necessary for selling a book? That's really difficult to answer, for there are precedents showing that some books sell very well without the author or the publisher lifting a finger to promote it. One of my first books, *The Well Body Book*, sold nearly a quarter of a million copies and was published in five languages with little help from my coauthor and me, or our publisher, to promote it. On the other hand, I've written books that sold far less than that even though they received considerable promotion.

Wherever you begin, do it in the name of bringing the benefits of your work to a broader number of people. And never forget that your publisher is your partner in all of this. Be of service to your readers, but do so with the perspective of keeping the circle of energy moving, honoring the fact that the energy that you give must bring energy back to sustain the work you are doing in the world.

Chapter Eleven

Closing Thoughts

> *The spiritual journey is the soul's life commingling with ordinary life.*
>
> —Christina Baldwin, *Calling the Circle*

Writing and publishing, like anything else in the world, can have a very long or a very short learning curve. And I am often reminded of how different we all are in terms of the life paths we are given. I'd venture to say that writing and publishing have presented some of the greatest spiritual lessons of my life—from learning patience and forgiveness to finding the courage to embrace my own gifts and honor my own voice. Ultimately, I suppose, there is no better way to move forward in our careers as writers than to do so as if each moment were an opportunity to learn not just the practical lessons of writing but the broader lessons of our own spiritual development.

The journey that begins with writing a book, then seeking an agent or publisher, and finally seeing your book in the bookstore may be one of the more challenging ones of your life. Along the way you'll surely come face to face with the hard realities of the real world. For example, on the way to getting published you may have to confront rejection by agents and publishers. In fact, this is more the rule than the exception. It's often said that most books are rejected a dozen or more times before finding the right publisher. For that reason, if no other, you can remind yourself to be philosophical about the turndowns. Remind yourself that you're in good company.

In truth, there are infinite reasons for an editor's or agent's rejection of a project. For example, I always warn new authors to carefully research agents and publishers before sending them anything. If you send a spiritual book project to an agent whose specialty is murder mysteries, the outcome is quite predictable. And if you send that same manuscript to a spiritual book publisher who already has all the new projects it can handle for the next three years, the rejection you receive will have nothing to do with the quality or importance of what you've written. While your closest friend or your psychic may assure you that the right publisher or agent is just around the next corner, you still have to deal with the day-to-day realities of a lot of other peoples' lives, and it may take a while for all those diverse energies to come together for you.

Always keep in mind that the creative powers within us are both very powerful and very fragile. Long ago, I was reminded by a teacher of mine that the creative gifts we each hold are, in fact, not our private property but simply another manifestation of the Divine Ground in which we all live. We are here to serve this larger reality through exercising this gift, and we cannot always know what Spirit intends for us in putting this creative power into our hands. Nevertheless, when we are our most creative, we draw from the very ground of our being, from our hearts. We deeply value what we have done, and to have what we've created be rejected can indeed be very painful. At such times I need to remind myself that the greater purpose of my efforts is yet to be revealed to me and that I need not see momentary disappointments along the way as defeats. We do not know what will happen tomorrow, so it behooves us to be careful to love the now and not judge ourselves.

I have had many positive surprises in my life in publishing. One of my more successful books, for example, was rejected twenty-some times before finding its publisher—and three of those rejections were by the same company that finally published it! As my wonderful teacher always reminds me, "Count on the surprises and you won't be disappointed!" Not that I always remember to follow his advice.

I am sure that if you are reading this book you already know that writing, in and of itself, has its own incomparable rewards. Publishing is surely one of them, but through the act of writing, and discovering the power of words, our own life experiences sometimes take on new light, revealing truths that take us closer to our spiritual identity. Sharing such words with others can be exquisite, and whether you publish and sell a million books or you read a special passage to a friend, that experience can be life-transforming for yourself as well as your readers.

Writing with the idea of publishing is important for several reasons. The first is obvious, of course: It's important to reach large numbers of people with your message. But it is also important at a personal level. For example, when you start thinking in terms of your words reaching thousands of people, you are stretched to think outside the limits of everyday communication. You also start thinking in terms of how your words will impact others' lives. There are great spiritual lessons in this. We begin seeking the universal themes and issues through which we bond as one. In the language of the perennial philosophy, we seek and find the Divine Ground and even experience it directly through our writing. To write for a large readership—meaning any number more than a dozen or so—we become more acutely attuned to what it means to be articulate about our beliefs. In the process we find our true voice and revel in the music we feel within our own hearts.

I mention the special gifts of writing as a reminder you can rely on during those dark times of doubt when the writing becomes particularly difficult and you need to remember your mission. At these times, accept the challenges you are receiving. Assume they are gifts and treat them accordingly, seeking the lessons they contain. Writing a book can never be a waste of time, whether it is ever published or not. What's true more often than not is that getting published requires a great deal of tenacity, but what fuels this tenacity is the realization that perhaps the greatest gifts are in the doing itself, in the act of writing and the many rewards it offers. Meanwhile, it is good to be reminded of Henry David Thoreau's words, penned nearly 150 years ago:

Closing Thoughts

> If one advances confidently in the direction of his dreams, and endeavors to live the life which he has imagined, he will meet with a success unexpected in common hours.[1]

Success doesn't come without the work and tenacity that writing requires, of course, but hopefully this book has contributed to making your journey easier and perhaps shortening your path to publication.

Resources for Writers

Twelve Spirit-Friendly Literary Agents

There are several thousand literary agents listed on the Internet, so how do you choose one that is effective and, more importantly, legitimate? What do I mean by "legitimate"? Unfortunately, there are people around who prey on inexperienced authors. They advertise themselves as agents but then want to charge exorbitant reading fees, or they tell you that they can edit your manuscript to make it publishable. Because some agents offer similar services, it's difficult to tell who is legit and who isn't. The easiest test is to request a list of books the agency has placed with publishers over the past year or two. If they're legit, they won't mind telling you. Some agents will even supply you with a list of their current clients, and if they're legit there will be a few on that list that you recognize. If they give you names you don't recognize, look up their books on Amazon.com and see what comes up on an Internet search of each name.

To check up on a literary agent you may have heard about,

peruse the website called "Editors and Preditors" at www.anotherealm.com/prededitors.

In recent years, a few excellent agents have begun charging reading fees, but they also supply you with a written evaluation of the work in return. And they are open and clear about why they are doing this. For example, two that I know of—who are highly successful agents—charge a reading fee because they believe that there are new writers around who definitely have something to contribute but who are collecting a lot of rejection slips without knowing why. (Most agents don't have the time to give you a long, free explanation of what you might do to make your manuscript acceptable.) If an agent explains this and also has a good list of projects she has sold to well-known, royalty-paying publishers, have a chat with her, look over any contracts or other literature she may send you, and then make a decision about whether or not you want to work with her.

All of the agents I list here are people I know or have worked with or who have been enthusiastically recommended by friends and clients. All of them are people with excellent track records in terms of the authors they represent and their sales to well-known, royalty-paying publishers.

Before seeing your manuscript, most agents want to get a query letter from you first, describing your work. This should always be no more than a single page, single-spaced and with 1.25-inch right and left margins and 1-inch margins at the top and bottom. I usually recommend sending one chapter to read as well. If an agent has a website (many don't), check there for that agent's particular submission guidelines. If there's no website, you can assume that a query letter with a single sample chapter is your best approach. Many agents prefer not to be queried by phone.

By the way, agents used to require a SASE (self-addressed, stamped envelope) so that they could return your query letter and sample chapter(s) if they weren't interested. With postage as high as it is these days, it's sometimes cheaper to let the recipient shred the pages you send while you print out new ones. Hopefully, the agent you send your material to will recycle the paper. Always consider this when sending a query. If you are not going to send a SASE, tell the agent they can shred and recycle your material. When you send whole manuscripts or longer proposals, it's usually worth the money to include a SASE.

Barbara Neighbors Deal Literary Associates. This agency specializes in health, personal growth, and spiritual development books. Query by email or regular mail with a one-page letter. (Barbara was my agent on this book and has an excellent client list, so I know she's good.) Write to: 125 Storm Way, Crescent City, CA 95531. Phone: (707) 458-3382. Email: BarbaraDeal@charter.net.

Bleecker Street Associates, Inc. Founded in 1984 by Agnes Birnbaum, who brought sixteen years in the book business to her work, this agency has an interest in spiritual and New Age nonfiction. Query first with a short letter describing the book and why you feel you're the right person to write it. Like many other agents and publishers, Agnes is particularly interested in authors who are eager to promote their work. Write to: 532 La Guardia Place, New York, NY 10012. Phone: (212) 677-4492.

Carol Mann Agency. This agency was founded in 1977 and has an excellent reputation. They handle a wide cross-section of books, including literary fiction, narrative nonfiction, popular psychology, some memoirs, and spirituality. Send a query letter with a card for sending you a reply. Write to: 55 Fifth Avenue, New York, NY 10003. Phone: (212) 206 5635.

Elizabeth Puttick Literary Agency. This is a small agency in London, England. While I don't know a lot about them, the lists of publishers they've sold to, as well as their list of authors, indicates this is a good contact. I list it here because there have been a number of books that have first sold to publishers in Great Britain prior to being published in the United States. Also, if you're an author in England, you'll especially value this contact. The Puttick website includes good information to check out. And they offer a service to help you revise a manuscript or proposal. They specialize in general nonfiction, with particular interests in self-help, Mind Body Spirit, health, women's issues, and business. Write to: 46 Brookfield Mansions, London, N6 6AT, United Kingdom. Email: agency@puttick.com Website: www.puttick.com.

Jeff and Deborah Herman, Jeff Herman Agency. The Hermans specialize in most areas of adult nonfiction, with a strong interest in personal growth, self-help, popular psychology, and popular business books. Write to: 332 Bleecker Street, Suite G31, New York, NY 10014. Phone: (212) 941-0540. Email: jeff@jeffherman/com.

Larsen-Pomada Literary Agency. This agency is one of the busiest on the West Coast. Michael Larsen and his partner, Elizabeth Pomada, represent a wide range of books, from business to spirituality. Michael is the author of *How to Write a Book Proposal,* as well as *Literary Agents: How to Get and Work with the Right One for You,* which I cite in "Books for Going Further," following. Query letter first. Write to: 1029 Jones Street, San Francisco, CA 94109. Phone: (415) 673-0939. Email: Larsenpoma@aol.com.

Loretta Barrett Books, Inc. Prior to starting her literary agency, Loretta was editor-in-chief of Anchor Books and vice president and executive editor at Doubleday & Co. While her agency represents literary novelists, scholars, and political figures, she also handles self-help and spiritual books. Your first contact with her should be with a well-written and succinct query letter. Write to: 101 Fifth Avenue, 11th Floor, New York, NY 10003. Phone: (212) 242-3420.

Natasha Kern Literary Agency. Though located in Portland, Oregon, this agency represents writers in virtually every state. The lists of authors and books they've placed is impressive, and they are seeking authors of spiritual books. Send queries by mail only. Do not email or query by phone. Write to: P.O. Box 2908, Portland, OR 97208. Website: www.natashakern.com.

Pam Bernstein & Associates. Pam has an impressive list of spiritual writers whom she represents. She established her agency in 1993 after a long and successful career as an agent with the William Morris Agency. While I haven't worked directly with her, three friends, one of them another literary agent, have recommended her. Query first with a brief (one-page) letter. Write to: 790 Madison Avenue, Suite 310, New York, NY 10021. Phone: (212) 288-1700.

Roger Jellinek, Jellinek & Murray Literary Agency. Founded in 1995, this agency represents some fifty clients in general adult fiction and nonfiction. Query first. Then, if query is accepted, send a minimal synopsis, table of contents, and the first two complete chapters. Write to: 2024 Mauna Place, Honolulu, HI 96822. Phone: (808) 521-4057. Email: Jellinek@lava.net.

Sarah J. Freyman Literary Agency. In business since the 1970s, Sarah Freyman represents a wide range of authors. She enjoys working with authors with well-grounded spiritual books. Query with a letter. Write to: 59 West 71st Street, Suite 9B, New York, NY 10023. Phone: (212) 362-9277.

Thomas Grady Agency. Established in 1997, this agency specializes in nonfiction in the areas of religion, spirituality, personal growth, biography, and memoir. I first met Tom when he was the editor-in-chief at Harper San Francisco and enjoyed working with him on two or three projects. He has worked in trade-book publishing for almost twenty-five years. Current clients include Sylvia Boorstein, Phil Cousineau, Andrew Harvey, and Huston Smith. Tom says, "Please read Inquiries About Representation on my website before submitting material." Write to: 209 Bassett Street, Petaluma, CA 94952. Phone: (707) 765-6229. Email: Tom@tgrady.com. Website: www.tgrady.com.

Publishers Seeking Spiritual Books

The following is my personal list of publishers. Most are publishers I have worked with directly, either as an author or as a freelance editor, so I can recommend them from firsthand experience. A few have been recommended by clients and friends whose experience and good sense I trust. Note, however, that there are many other publishers out there, both large New York houses and independents, located throughout the country, that are publishing spiritual books. Just because they don't appear on my list doesn't mean they aren't good; it just means I haven't had experience with them yet. Had I listed them all, I would have been duplicating the work of other encyclopedic listings such as *Literary Market Place, Writers Yearbook,* or *Jeff Herman's Guide to Book Publishers, Editors and Literary Agents.* My list is one I would make up for a close friend who asks me for my personal recommendations. That said, I believe this is an excellent place to start shopping for publishers. Just keep in mind that your search can and probably should extend beyond this list.

Bantam Dell Publishing Group. This is one of the largest mainstream houses that publishes popular spiritual, religious, and New Age titles. They accept unagented queries of a page or so, along with an author bio. Write to: 1540 Broadway, New York, NY 10036. Phone: (212) 782-9000. Website: www.randomhouse.com/bantamdell.

Bear & Company. The main focus of this house is Native American and Earth-based spirituality. Originally based in Santa Fe, New Mexico, they have joined with Inner Traditions and now are based in Vermont. Query with letter, bio, and return card and SASE. Write to: P.O. Box 388, Rochester, VT 05767. Phone: (802) 767-3174. Website: www.innertraditions.com/bearpress.htm.

Celestial Arts (also includes Crossing Press and Ten Speed Press). I've had a long-time association with this publisher and have published several books with them myself. My main contact there is Veronica (Fuzzy) Randall, senior editor for Celestial Arts. In the past few years, Celestial acquired Crossing Press, which specializes in Native American and practical spirituality. Both companies are imprints of Ten Speed Press. Query first or work with an agent. Write to: 999 Harrison Street, Berkeley, CA 94710. Phone: (510) 559-1600. Website: www.tenspeed.com

Conari Press. This company started in Berkeley, California, and was acquired by Red Wheel/Weiser in the past few years. While they focus on women's issues, they also are interested in books on personal transformation and spirituality. Query first or work with an agent. Write to: Conari Press/Red Wheel/Weiser, 368 Congress Street, Boston, MA 92210. Phone: (617) 542-1324. Website: www.conari.com

Dutton Plume. Perhaps the best-known spiritual book published by this house in recent years is James Van Praagh's *Reaching to Heaven: A Spiritual Journey Through Life and Death*. As an imprint of Penguin/Putnam publishing group, Dutton Plume prefers agented manuscripts. They publish many books on spiritual and personal development, so get an agent and give them a try. Write to: 375 Hudson Street, New York, NY 10014. Phone: (212) 366-2000. Website: www.penguinputnam.com

Hampton Roads. My own book, *Spirit Animals and the Wheel of Life: Earth-Centered Practices for Daily Living,* is published with this company. They specialize in spiritual and metaphysical books that help people develop themselves spiritually and psychologically. They pioneered the genre now known as "visionary fiction," that is, novels with a spiritual or metaphysical theme. It's best to work with agent. Write to: 1125 Stoney Ridge Road, Charlottesville, VA 22902. Phone: (804) 296-2772. Website: www.hamptonroadspub.com.

HarperCollins/Harper San Francisco. This is one of the largest mainstream houses that specializes in spiritual and popular religious books. I've published with them twice, with my books *Zuni Fetishes: Using Native American Objects for Meditation, Reflection, and Insight* and *The Holotropic Mind,* which I coauthored. I've also worked with other authors who are published there, so I can recommend this publisher highly. It's best to work with an agent. Write to: 353 Sacramento Street, Suite 500, San Francisco, CA. Phone: (415) 477-4400. Website: www.harpercollins.com.

Health Communications. Best known in recent years for the *Chicken Soup for the Soul* books, this is a large, independent publisher with a solid publishing program. They cover everything from books for teenagers to adult self-help, New Age, health, diet, and spirituality. They're open to queries by authors. Write to: 3201 S.W. 15th Street, Deerfield Beach, FL 33442. Phone: (800) 441-5569. Website: www.hcibooks.com.

H.J. Kramer. This publisher is now an imprint with New World Library, though they maintain their editorial autonomy. Best known for publishing Dan Millman's bestselling spiritual novel, *Way of The Peaceful Warrior,* the books of John Robbins, and the channeled books of *Sanaya Roman,* the Kramers are presently focusing attention on children's books. Query first. Write to: 14 Pamaron Way, Novato, CA 94949. Phone: (800) 972-6657. Website: www.nwlib.com.

Inner Ocean Publishing, Inc. This is the publisher of the same book you now hold in your hand. I've thoroughly enjoyed working with them, both as an author and in my role as an editor. I hope to continue this association for many years to come. Their focus is on books that contribute to the spiritual evolution of people everywhere. Query first. Write to: P.O. Box 1239, Makawao, HI 96768-1239. Phone: (898) 573-8000. Website: www.inner ocean.com.

Inner Traditions. You've already learned a little about Inner Traditions if you read my write-up on Bear & Company. They publish a wide range of books about the spiritual traditions of the world, both Eastern and Western. They like books that bring spirituality and transformation down to earth, with practical applications and wisdom for our everyday lives. Write to: P.O. Box 388, Rochester, VT 05767. Phone: (802) 767-3174. Website: www.innertraditions.com.

J.P. Tarcher. Originally a West Coast publisher and now part of the Penguin/Putnam group of publishers, Tarcher has established a reputation for high-quality books by spiritual and personal growth authors. I've worked with them on several books, and they've always been great to work with. Their editor-in-chief,

Joel Fotinos, is a brilliant book person. I recommend working through an agent with this company. Write to: 375 Hudson Street, New York, NY 10014. Phone: (212) 366-2000. Website: www.penguinputnam.com.

Llewellyn Worldwide, Ltd. This may be one of the oldest spiritual book publishers in the business. Established in 1897, Llewellyn is well known for metaphysical, occult, New Age, and spiritual books. Their editorial preference tends toward books that are practical and that guide readers through the material so that they can easily apply the principles. The company has very specific guidelines to follow when submitting a manuscript. Be sure to download these from their website before submitting even a query letter. Write to: P.O. Box 64383, St. Paul, MN 55164-0383. Phone: (651) 291-1970. Website: www.llewellyn.com.

Marlowe & Company. I've worked with this publisher on two successful book projects, and they are great to work with. The managing editor, Matthew Lore, looks for books on spirituality, personal growth, self-help, and wellness. Address queries to him. Write to: 245 West 17th Street, 11th floor, New York, NY 10011-5300. Phone: (212) 981-9919. Website: www.marlowepub.com.

New World Library. Started in 1977 on a shoestring, New World Library is now one of the leading independent publishers of spiritual books. Their titles include *The Power of Now*, by Eckhart Tolle; *Seven Spiritual Laws of Success*, by Deepak Chopra; and

Creative Visualization, by Shakti Gawain. They publish my book *Write from the Heart*, and I've been involved with several other books they publish. So I know them well and recommend them highly. Write to: 14 Pamaron Way, Novato, CA 94949. Phone: (800) 972-6657. Website: www.nwlib.com.

Quest Books. This publisher is an imprint of the Theosophical Society of America. (Theosophy is the blending of philosophy, religion and science, seeking a vision of being at one with the universe.) Quest looks for spiritual self-help books, with particular interest in Eastern and Western religions, Native American spirituality, women's and men's spirituality, and books on theosophy. Writing must be excellent. They're not interested in personal awakening memoirs. Send queries or proposals. Write to: P.O. Box 270, Wheaton, IL 60198. Phone: (630) 665-0130. Website: www.theosophical.org.

Red Wheel/Weiser/Conari. The parent company, Samuel Weiser, pioneered the publication of books on Eastern religions in the early 1960s. They have since brought together Red Wheel and Conari, to create an excellent venue for spiritual and personal growth books, along with more scholarly works on Eastern spiritual practices. Again, this is a publisher I've worked with and I like them a lot. Query first or work with an agent. Write to: Conari Press/Red Wheel/Weiser, 368 Congress Street, Boston, MA 92210. Phone: (617) 542-1324. Website: www.redwheelweiser.com.

Simon & Schuster. This is a large New York house, publishing virtually everything imaginable. I've worked with them on at least one successful project, and in spite of their size their editors have enough autonomy to make it seem like you're working with a much smaller house. Their list of spiritual and personal growth books is extensive. Work with an agent. They take few unsolicited manuscripts. Write to: 1230 Avenue of the Americas, New York, NY 10020. Phone: (212) 698-7000. Website: www.SimonSays.com.

Fifty-Six Bookstores That Welcome Authors

Keep this list in mind when you are ready to put together a publicity campaign for your book. These are all bookstores that I've either had personal contact with or that I have heard about from other authors, clients, or publicists. They welcome author visits and host mini-workshops or author lectures in their stores. (See the "Books for Going Further" section, following, to delve further into ways to promote your work.)

To make use of this list, consider sending postcards with a graphic of your book's cover, a short description of its contents, ordering information, and endorsements. Your publisher may help you with this. Sometimes the publisher will even pick up the printing bill and do all the mailings. (Look in the "Printers and Other Services" section, following, to find information about printers who will prepare full-color postcard announcements.)

Resources for Writers

These are your core contacts for setting up in-store presentations and book signings. Be sure to share this list with your publisher's publicist, who may wish to add these addresses to his or her own list of publicity contacts.

Alaska

Fireside Books, 720 South Alaska Street, Palmer, 99645, ph (907)745-2665

California

Black Oak Books, 1491 Shattuck Avenue, Berkeley, 94709, ph (510) 486-0698

Bodhi Tree Bookstore, 8585 Melrose Avenue, West Hollywood, 90069-5199, ph (310) 659-1733

Book Passage, 51 Tamal Vista Boulevard, Corte Madera, 94925, ph (415) 927-0960

Book Soup, 8818 Sunset Boulevard, Los Angeles, 90069, ph (310) 659-3110

Chaucer & Co. Bookstore, 3321 State Street, Santa Barbara, 93105-2623 ph (805) 682-4067

Cody's Books, 2454 Telegraph Avenue, Berkeley, 94704, ph (510) 845-7852

East West Bookshop, 324 Castro Street, Mountain View, 94041-1297, ph (650) 988-9800

Hennessey & Ingalis, 1254 3rd Street Promenade, Santa Monica, 90401, ph (310) 458-9074

Phoenix Bookstore, 1514 Fifth Street, Santa Monica, 90401, ph (310) 395-9516

Colorado

Tattered Cover, 1536 Wynkoop Street, Denver, 80202, ph (303) 322-7727

District of Columbia

Olsson's Books & Records, 1307 19th Street NW, Washington, D. C., 20007, ph (202) 785-1133

Georgia

Phoenix and the Dragon, 5531 Roswell Road, Atlanta, 30342, ph (404) 255-5207

Waterstone's, 3200 Windy Hill Road SE, Atlanta, 30339

Idaho

Bookpeople, 512 South Main Street, Moscow, 83843, ph (208) 882-7957

Illinois

Transitions Bookplace, 1000 West North Avenue, Chicago, 60622, ph (312) 951-7323

Massachusetts

Book Loft, Barrington Plaza, Great Barrington, 01230, ph (413) 528-1521

Jabberwocky, 50 Water Street, Newburyport, 01950, ph (978) 465-9359

Michigan

Crazy Wisdom Bookstore, 206 North 4th Avenue, Ann Arbor, 48104, ph (313) 665-2757

Store for Miracle Minded, 11200 East Eleven Mile Road, Warren, 48089, ph (810) 758-3050

Minnesota

Hungry Mind, 1648 Grand Avenue, St. Paul, 55105, ph (651) 699-0587

Kmitsch Girls, 324 South Main Street, Stillwater, 55082, ph (612) 430-1827

Nevada

Sundance Bookstore, 1155 West 4th Street, Reno, 89503, ph (775) 786-1188

New Hampshire

Toadstool Bookshop, 12 Depot Square, Peterborough, 03458, ph (603) 924-3543

Water Street Bookstore, 125 Water Street, Exeter, 03833, ph (603) 778-9731

New Mexico

Ark Bookstore, 133 Romero Street, Santa Fe, 87501, ph (505) 988-3709

Page One, 11018 Montgomery NE, Albuquerque, 87111, ph (505) 294-2026

New York

Asia Society, 725 Park Avenue, New York, 10021, ph (212) 288-6400

Books & Co., 939 Madison Avenue, New York, 10021, ph (212) 737-1450

Coliseum Books, 1771 Broadway, New York, 10019, ph (212) 757-8103

East-West Books, 568 Columbus Avenue, New York, 10024, ph (212) 787-7552

Nahani, 482 Broadway, Sarasota Springs, 12866, ph (518) 587-4322

New York Open Center, 83 Spring Street, New York, 10012, ph (212) 219-2527

Omega Bookstore, 260 Lake Drive, Rhinebeck, 12572, ph (914) 266-4222

Rizzoli Bookstores, 300 Park Avenue South, 3rd Floor, New York, 10010, ph (212) 387-3400

St. Marks Bookshop, 31 Third Avenue, New York, 10003, ph (212) 260-7853

Ohio

Delphic Books, 1793 Coventry Road, Cleveland Heights, 44118, ph (216) 321-8106

Joseph-Beth Booksellers, 2692 Madison Road, Cincinnati, 45208, ph (513)731-7770

Learned Owl, 204 North Main, Hudson, 44236, ph (330) 653-2252

Nickleby's Bookstore Café, 1425 Grandview Avenue, Columbus, 43212, ph (614) 488-2665

Ontario, Canada

World's Biggest Bookstore, 20 Edwards Street, Toronto, Ontario, Canada, M5G 1C9, ph (416) 977-7009

Oregon

Jackson's Books, 320 Liberty Street SE, Salem, 97301, ph (503) 399-8694

New Renaissance Books, 1338 NW 23rd Avenue, Portland, 97210, ph (503) 224-4929

Soundpeace, 199 East Main Street, Ashland, 97520, ph (541) 482-3633

Pennsylvania

Journey of Life, 810 Bellefonte Street, Pittsburgh, 15232, ph (412) 681-8755

Robin's Book Store, 108 South 13th St., Philadelphia, 19107, ph (215)735-1795

Texas

Body, Mind, Spirit, 4344 Westheimer, Houston, 77027, ph (713) 993-0550

Bookpeople, 603 North Lamar Boulevard, Austin, 78703, ph (512) 472-4288

Shakespeare Beethoven, 13350 Callas Parkway, Dallas, 75240, ph (214) 387-1720

Voertmans, 1314 West Hickory, Denton, 76201, ph (817) 387-1313

Vermont

Chassman & Bem, Ltd., 81 Church Street, Burlington, 05401, ph (802) 862-4332

Washington

Aunties Bookstore, 402 West Main, Spokane, 99201, ph (888) 802-6657

Eagle Harbor Book Co., 157 Winslow Way East, Bainbridge Island, 98110, ph (206) 842-5332

East-West Books, 6500 Roosevelt Avenue NE, Seattle, 98115, ph (206) 523-3726

Elliot Bay Books, 101 South Main Street, Seattle, 98104, ph (503) 399-6600

Village Books, 1210 Eleventh Street, Bellingham, 98225, ph (360) 671-2626

Websites for Writers

Increasingly, we writers are going to the Internet for help on grammar, research of topics, quotes from other authors, and general information about publishing. There is almost too much to choose from along these lines. For that reason, I've sorted through hundreds of writers' websites looking for the ones that I find most useful. I chose the following sites for what they offer writers in terms of the skills of the craft, the depth of their research materials, and their professional understanding of publishing. I found many websites that offered chat lines for writers and was disappointed with the quality of information most of them put out. While it is useful for writers to talk with other writers, what too often happens is that there are always a few who speak with great authority about publishing but whose information and experience mostly come from less than dependable resources. The misinformation they put out certainly does not serve beginning writers well. So beware. Protect yourself by looking for the qualifications of the people offering free advice. Unless they've published at least two books with well-known publishers, take what they say with a grain of salt. That said, peruse the following websites. Get to know what they offer and log the ones you find useful onto your favorites list.

Absolute Write

www.absolutewrite.com

This site offers good resources for writers in general, though no focus on spiritual writing per se. Go here for articles and tips for writers; a free newsletter; lists of literary agents, editors, and publishers; a chat line with other authors; and community sharing. It was originally focused only on screenwriting, but now it's not limited to that.

Amazon

www.amazon.com

Most of us think of this as a place to order books. It's also a good place for getting information such as: Is there already a book by the title I chose for mine? Is the subject I'm writing about popular or unpopular? (Look for the "Amazon Sales Rank." The smaller the number, the higher the sales.) Amazon is even working on a database that will enable you to search the text of most of the books they carry! Search categories to find out where your book fits in. (Categories are universalized in the book business.)

American Booksellers Association

www.bookweb.org

I believe it's important for authors to know a little about everything that affects the production and sale of their books. So visit this site and read about the concerns of independent booksellers, that is, smaller book stores that are not associated with chains such as Borders or Barnes & Noble. The independents are important, since that's where the bulk of your books will probably be sold.

Bartleby

www.bartleby.com

This is a very useful site for looking up quotes and doing research. It offers access or links to an encyclopedia, dictionaries, and a thesaurus, as well as collections of fiction, nonfiction, poetry, and history.

Book Market – John Kremer

www.bookmarket.com

A website for authors who are looking for ways to promote their books, Book Market was put together by John Kremer, author of *1001 Ways to Market Your Books* and teacher of workshops on marketing. While Kremer's main target is small publishers, most of the marketing ideas are also useful for authors with bigger houses. It's worth looking at, but if you get some ideas for promoting your book, make sure you coordinate your efforts with your publisher.

Creativity for Life

www.creativity.com

Check in here for articles on stimulating your creativity—you can even contribute an article if you've come up with some genius way to keep the creative juices flowing.

Hal Zina Bennett

ww.halzinabennett.com

I might as well get a plug for myself in here. Six to eight times a year I publish new articles reflecting on writing and publishing. I archive a number of these on my website—all free of charge.

Literary Market Place

www.literarymarketplace.com

Literary Market Place, also known as LMP, has long been the main source for finding out about publishers. You can search, for example, for publishers who specialize in spiritual books. You'll get names of editors at those houses, in addition to addresses, phone numbers, etc. It's really the best place to go if you are searching for a specific type of publisher, a literary agent, or even a lecture agent. It's by subscription—several hundred dollars per year. However, there's now a special subscription rate of $20 for a week's worth of research—plenty of time for you to find out what you need.

PearlSoup

www.pearlsoup.com

This is a community of writers sharing personal experiences. It's a good place to go for anecdotes, and if you use a person's story, of course, be sure to get permission—in writing!

Preditors & Editors

www.anotherealm.com/prededitors

This website is mostly known for its warnings about scams by certain agents and editors who feed off inexperienced writers. There's a large community sharing information about scams that can hurt writers—but also good information on agents and publishers who are legit, tips on writing query letters and proposals, and links to other useful sites.

Shaw Guides

www.shawguides.com

People looking for workshops to attend often find themselves perusing what's available at Shaw Guides. If you are going to put together a workshop to go along with your book, consider listing here. To check out how it works, go to the website and on the first menu click on "High Performance Programs." You'll then see a "Search Hints" box. Type in "Personal growth." You'll be taken to a list of workshops presently listed. Perusing them, you'll see how you might put together your own ad. This is a good way to build a mailing list, since people will be sending you emails to find out more about you. I get about fifty requests a month from Shaw Guides for information about my workshops.

The Soul Food Café

www.dailywriting.net

Don't miss this one. This is a beautifully put together forum for writers. You'll find everything from writing exercises to stretch and strengthen your creativity muscles to information on putting together a website. You've got to visit this site to fully appreciate its offerings.

U.S. Copyright Office

www.copyright.gov

Here's everything you need to know—and then some—about copyrights. You can also download a number of government publications, including how to apply to copyright your manuscript. Keep in mind, however, that your publisher will do all this for you. Prior to publication, protect your work by putting a copyright notice on your manuscript. (Copyright © 2005 by Name of author.)

Westegg

www.westegg.com

This is a good resource for finding quotes, especially clichés, and for tracing the etymology of words.

WritersDigest.Com

www.writersdigest.com

As the name implies, this is *Writers Digest*'s official website. There's much information here, including access (for a price) to the magazine, chat lines, writer's online workshops, the latest offerings of the Writers Digest Book Club, their bookstore, and great lists.

WritersNet

www.writers.net

You'll find this a good place to network with other writers about writing and publishing. There's information here about literary agents, publishers, and other online resources. Visit and browse.

Writers Write

www.writerswrite.com

This site offers writing and publishing news, with a message board, interviews, job listings and good links to other websites that should interest writers.

Professional Associations for Writers

Once you're a published author—and sometimes before—you can join a professional association that offers a wide range of benefits and news about the publishing business, slanted especially toward the needs of authors.

The Association of Authors and Publishers (AAP). This is a nonprofit association of authors (you don't have to be published), editors, designers, artists, printers, publishers, marketers, distributors, booksellers, Internet professionals—and anybody associated with the writing, publishing, distribution, or marketing of books. This is an excellent networking association, providing up-to-date information through workshop announcements and a newsletter. Website: www.authorsandpublishers.org.

Authors Guild. This is the oldest and largest association for published authors in the United States. The guild is instrumental in lobbying for authors' rights and even going to court for us when necessary. They've been instrumental in writing approved publishing contracts and have a legal department to help advise authors of their rights by reviewing contracts. They publish a quarterly report with informative articles for authors. Recently, they established a website service where an author can easily build his own informative website and maintain that site at a ridiculously low fee to members. Write to: 31 East 28th Street, New York, NY 10016. Phone: (212) 563-5904.
Website: www.authorsguild.org.

Canadian Authors Association (CAA). Founded in 1921, Canada's national writing association has played an important part in developing and supporting the Canadian writing community. Registered as a National Arts Service Organization, it has a charitable status (similar to nonprofit status in the United States).
Website: www.canauthors.org.

National Association of Women Writers. This is a nonprofit organization founded in 2001 to develop a network where women writers can inspire, motivate, and teach each other through publications, workshops, and conferences. Membership is open to all women writers regardless of past publications.
Website: www.naww.org.

National Writers Union (NWU). This is the trade union for freelance writers associated with American publishers or employers. With a collected strength of 6,500 members, NWU is committed to improving the economic and working conditions of writers. The NWU is a modern, innovative union offering grievance resolution, industry campaigns, contract advice, health and dental plans, member education, job banks, networking, social events, and much more. NWU is affiliated with the United Automobile Workers (UAW) and, through them, with the AFL-CIO.
Website: www.nwu.org.

Books for Going Further

How to Write a Book Proposal (3rd Edition), **by Michael Larsen. Writers Digest Books, 2004. $15.99.** I recommend that you shop around for the third edition. While the other editions are good, many things have changed in publishing between the second and third edition. This book contains profuse instructions as well as model proposals to follow.

Jeff Herman's Guide to Book Publishers, Editors and Literary Agents 2004: Who They Are! What They Want! and How to Win Them Over!, **by Jeff Herman. Writers, 2003. $29.95.** This is just what the title and subtitle say it is. Besides listing publishers, editors, and literary agents, Herman includes excellent articles by publishing professionals. It's well worth the money for the insiders' perspective that's offered here.

***Literary Agents: What They Do, How They Do It, and How to Find and Work with the Right One for You*, revised and updated by Michael Larsen. John Wiley & Sons, 2003. $15.95.** This is as entertaining and witty as it is informative. By a veteran agent who's also the author and coauthor of eleven books, it covers everything from how to find an agent to how to write a query letter. It's valuable to get information about literary agents from a literary agent. Michael is straightforward about what excites him about a book and what turns him off.

***Publicize Your Book!: An Insider's Guide to Getting Your Book the Attention It Deserves*, by Jacqueline Deval. Perigee Books, 2003. $15.95.** I've found this to be one of the easiest-to-use marketing books for authors. It includes sections on writing a marketing plan, developing a press kit, working with a publicist, getting magazine and newspaper coverage, Internet marketing, prepping for interviews, setting up bookstore appearances, and lots more.

***Write from the Heart: Unleashing the Power of Your Creativity*, by Hal Zina Bennett.** New World Library, 2001. $14.00. In this book I've presented material that has grown out of writing seminars I've taught over the past fifteen years. Departing from the usual craft-oriented book, I describe a unique process I developed over my thirty-plus years in publishing and teaching to help authors find their true voice and the wellspring of their own creativity. There are quotes, exercises, and highlighted "Core Concepts" to provide what amounts to a self-directed seminar.

***Write the Perfect Book Proposal: Ten That Sold and Why (2nd Edition)*, by Jeff and Deborah Herman. John Wiley & Sons, 2001. $15.95.** This book gives comprehensive instructions for writing a successful book proposal and contains ten models of proposals that were successful, getting their authors excellent contracts.

Printers and Other Services

Because so much responsibility for promotion rests on the authors' shoulders these days, we writers need to become our own public relations experts—and sometimes that's going to mean putting out our own money and time to let people know about our books. Sometimes that will mean sending flyers and picture postcards to potential buyers, particularly bookstores, and particularly independent bookstores such as I have listed previously. Maybe you'll put together a workshop on the same subject as your book, and you'll want to send out flyers to potential students. For that, you'll need a high-quality printer. I've listed two here that give excellent service. (Be sure to check with your publisher first.)

Printers for Brochures and Postcards

TU-Vets Printing. This company specializes in flyers and postcards. Check out their website, email, or call for complete, current price lists. Write to: 5635 East Beverly Boulevard, Los Angeles, CA 90022. Call Henry Ayala: (800) 894-8977. Email: tuvets@aol.com Website: www.tuvets.com.

TWIG: This company prints a variety of promotional items, from brochures to bookmarks to flyers and business cards. They also have promotional packages designed for books, including 5,000 each full-color bookmarks, postcards, and business cards for a very nominal fee. Phone: (561) 750-9901.
Website: www.twigonestop.com.

Publishers' Associations and Newsletters

Some of the best sources of promotional information for authors, whether you publish with a larger publisher or you self-publish, is from associations that are set up for small publishers. I list three of my favorites here.

Dan Poynter's Newsletter

Dan has been in the self-publishing business for at least a couple decades. He teaches workshops on everything from self-publishing to author promotion. Go to his website to sign up for his free newsletter. Not everything you see there will be for you if you are published with a large publisher, but the news is always important for anyone in the book business.
Website: www.parapub.com/news.html.

Publishers Marketing Association (PMA)

Again, the main purpose of this association is to serve independent publishers, and there is a membership fee of approximately $150 per year for nonpublishers. Besides access to information about what's going on in the book business, the benefits of joining this group range from group health insurance to seminars on marketing, and much more. See their website for complete information and current membership fees. Ask about discounts for affiliate members. Write to: 627 Aviation Way, Manhattan Beach, CA 90266. Phone: (310) 372-2732.
Website: www.pma-online.org.

Small Publishers Association of North America (SPAN)

Like PMA, SPAN was set up to serve small publishers. However, it offers a great amount of information about the book business that authors can make use of. National associations of this kind keep their fingers on the pulse of the national and international book scenes. Write to: P.O. Box 1306, Buena Vista, CO 81211. Phone: (719) 395-4790. Website: www.SPANnet.org.

About the Author

If you explore your own bookshelves carefully, and peruse the acknowledgment pages of your favorite books on health, personal growth, creativity, and spirituality, there's a good chance that you will find Hal's name there. He has helped other authors and publishers develop more than 200 books, many of which have become not only well known but well loved, making a positive difference in the lives of millions of people.

Besides ghost-writing, collaborating, and editing, he has more than thirty published books of his own to his credit. Along with coauthor Dr. Mike Samuels, he broke new ground with one of the first popular books that presented a complementary approach to holistic health: *The Well Body Book,* published by Random House in 1971 and now a classic. His other collaborations include *Follow Your Bliss,* coauthored with Susan J. Sparrow; *The Holotropic Mind,* with Stanislav Grof, M.D.; and *How to Write with a Collaborator,* with author-literary agent Michael Larsen.

Hal's independently authored books cover a wide range: *No More Public School,* on alternative education; *The Doctor Within,* on the self-healing capacities of our body-mind; *Spirit Animals and the Wheel of Life*, on developing a daily practice of Earth-based spirituality; *Spirit Circle*, a visionary novel exploring ancient spiritual teachings in contemporary life; and *Write from the Heart*, on tapping the powers of your creativity.

Throughout his long career Hal has dedicated himself to the expansion of our human capabilities for the betterment of our own lives, the lives of those around us, and our planet.

For more information, visit his website: www.HalZinaBennett.com.

Endnotes

Chapter One: Writing in Spirit

1. Stephen Nachmanovitch, *Free Play: Improvisation in Life and Art* (New York: Tarcher Books, 1990) 94
2. *The Perennial Philosophy.* (New York: Harper & Row, 1945)

Chapter Two: From Revelation to Publication

1. Stan & Christina are co-editors of "Spiritual Emergency: Understanding and Treatment of Transpersonal Crisis." (*Re-Vision Journal* 8:7, 1986)
2. Gerald G. Jampolsky and Diane Cirincione, *Change Your Mind, Change Your Life* (New York: Bantam, 1993) 123

Chapter Three: Know Your Mission

1. May Sarton, *At Seventy* (New York: W.W. Norton, 1984) 68

Endnotes

Chapter Four: Find Models to Follow

1. C.G. Jung, *Memories, Dreams, Reflections* (New York: Vintage Books, 1963) 183
2. Arthur Hastings, *With the Tongues of Men and Angels* (San Francisco: Holt, Rinehart & Winston, 1991) 1

Chapter Five: Mapping Out Your Book

1. Charles A. Garfield and Hal Zina Bennett, *Peak Performance: Mental Training Techniques of the World's Greatest Athletes* (Los Angeles: Tarcher, 1984) 44-60

Chapter Six: Fostering Receptivity and Change

1. Gabrielle Roth, *Maps to Ecstasy* (Novato: Nataraj Publishing, 1991) 92
2. Emmett E. Miller, *Deep Healing: The Essence of Mind/Body Medicine* (La Jolla: Hay House, 1997) 231
3. Hugh Prather, *Notes on How to Live in the World and Still Be Happy* (New York: Doubleday, 1986) 156
4. Katherine Q. Revoir, *Spiritual Doodles & Mental Leapfrogs: A Playbook for Unleashing Spiritual Self-Expression* (Boston: Red Wheel/Weiser, 1999) 42
5. Christina Baldwin, *Calling the Circle* (Newberg: Swan Raven, 1994) 15
6. Dawn Callan, *Awakening the Warrior Within* (Novato: Nataraj Publishing, 1995) 143

7. Don Gerrard, *One Bowl* (New York: Marlowe, 2001) 76

8. Hugh Prather, *Notes on How to Live in the World and Still Be Happy* (New York: Doubleday, 1986) 265

Chapter Seven: Exercises That Grab Your Readers' Attention

1. John Muir, *How to Keep Your Volkswagen Alive,* 2nd edition (Santa Fe: John Muir Publications) 23

2. Hal Zina Bennett, *Lens of Perception.* (Berkeley: Celestial Arts, 1994)

3. Eckhart Tolle, *The Power of Now: A Guide to Spiritual Enlightenment* (Novato: New World Library, 1999) 97

Chapter Eight: Where Your Journal Can Take You

1. Hugh Prather, *Notes to Myself* (New York: Bantam, 1983) 97-106

2. C.G. Jung, *Psychological Reflections: An Anthology of His Writings* (Princeton: Princeton University Press, 1953) 326

3. Gerald G. Jampolsky and Diane Cirincione, *Change Your Mind, Change Your Life* (New York: Bantam, 1993) 80

Chapter Nine: Getting Paid to Write Your Book

1. Paul H. Ray and Sherry Ruth Anderson, *The Cultural Creatives* (New York: Harmony Books, 2000)

Chapter Eleven: Closing Thoughts

1. Henry David Thoreau, *Walden* (New York: Dover Publications, 1995) 93